RESPONSIBLE DOG OWNERSHIP

The rewards of responsible dog ownership are well mirrored in this group of happy, secure and robust Norwegian Elkhounds. Dogs like these, which are loved, well looked after and raised to be the ideal companion dogs, serve as the example for which every dog owner should constantly strive.

RESPONSIBLE DOG OWNERSHIP

Kathy Diamond Davis

HOWELL
BOOK HOUSE

New York

Maxwell Macmillan Canada
Toronto

Maxwell Macmillan International
New York   Oxford   Singapore   Sydney

Howell Book House
Macmillan Publishing Company
866 Third Avenue
New York, NY 10022

Maxwell Macmillan Canada, Inc.
1200 Eglinton Avenue East
Suite 200
Don Mills, Ontario M3C 3N1

Macmillan Publishing Company is part of the Maxwell Communication Group of Companies.

Library of Congress Cataloging-in-Publication Data

Davis, Kathy Diamond.
    Responsible dog ownership / Kathy Diamond Davis.
        p.   cm.
    ISBN 0-87605-801-2
    1. Dogs.   2. Dog owners.   3. Human-animal relationships.
4. Animal welfare.   5. Responsibility.   I. Title.
SF427.D29   1994
636.7—dc20   93-17581
                                                                    CIP

Macmillan books are available at special discounts for bulk purchases for sales promotions, premiums, fund-raising, or educational use. For details, contact:

Special Sales Director
Macmillan Publishing Company
866 Third Avenue
New York, NY 10022

10 9 8 7 6 5 4 3 2 1

Printed in the United States of America

Contents

Foreword

RESPONSIBLE DOG OWNERSHIP, by Kathy Diamond Davis, should be required reading for every present and potential dog owner on Earth, as declared by me—that is, if I could have my way. This is only a dream, of course, but I feel so strongly about the helpful information put forth by Mrs. Davis that this is the only possible way to begin my introduction.

Sound dogmatic? Maybe so, but after working closely with dogs for over twenty years, the last ten plus years as a small animal veterinarian in the United States, I can tell you that we can all learn a great deal more on how to relate to our dogs. The goal: to form a lasting, healthy relationship for dog owner and loyal companion, a true best friend.

Very often the master link between the dog owner and dog will be either the breeder, professional dog trainer or veterinarian (or various combinations of all these). The reason is communication—we've all been conditioned in today's society to believe that proper communication can avoid or solve most problems at home, in the workplace and elsewhere. Here lies the enigma in dog ownership.

Just as confusing as it would be for us if we traveled to a foreign country without knowledge of the language, consider how it is for a dog coming into our household. Not only does the dog not know our lingo while depending on us for everything, but, more important, *we do not understand the dog's language.*

What's that? Dogs have a language? You bet they do! The canine is an extremely social being that in the wild often lives in well-organized, smoothly functioning packs. They communicate with each other via a multitude of behavioral signals involving body postures, sounds and smells.

When a new pet puppy or adult dog enters the home, people are not people in its eyes, but new pack members. Normally, there is a strong social hierarchy or pecking order among pack members. Individual personalities range from the strong dominant leader types to the more submissive, weaker and follower personalities, with a full gamut of personalities in between. If you don't understand the canine language, "cutesy" puppy behavior may be more significant than you think. In the puppy's eyes, these social cues it is giving you that are passing right over your head may actually mean a whole different thing as the dog positions itself in its new pack.

For instance, if a new pup has a dominant leader-type personality and the social cues it has been sending out since puppyhood come back unchallenged by the owner, it will grow up having a pack-leader mentality. This does not occur willfully on the owner's part, but occurs because all along the true meaning of much of the dog's behavioral signals has been misunderstood. So, as this dog grows to maturity, never having had its leadership role challenged, it may not think twice about growling, snarling—or worse, biting you or a family member to put the person back into his or her place if things are not going the dog's way. This is natural behavior and is typical of how leader dogs deal with subservient pack members in the wild.

If people understand dogs' signals, then they can communicate to them more effectively to establish desirable behavior patterns among their new pack members: me and you. This is the bottom line: those who know and love dogs and really understand them and their language experience the best relationships with their pets and vice versa. Everyone benefits in these loving relationships, dogs and owners alike.

One of the many hats I wear as a veterinary practitioner is that of psychologist/psychiatrist, counseling canine owners on how to solve one crisis management or behavior problem after another. This, mind you, is not medicine, but rather, communication skills that require improving between pets and people.

Responsible dog ownership starts even before a dog is acquired. You must give careful consideration to some key questions: Why do you want a dog? Who will take care of it after the novelty of the new family addition wears off? Where will the dog live, inside or outside, and how will you keep the dog from roaming? What are the day-to-day, month-to-month, year-to-year responsibilities of health care and maintenance? When is the best time in your life to provide for the dog in both commitment and finances?

After thoughtfully considering these questions, you must then decide what breed or type of dog to obtain. It is very practical to suit the breed, size and personality of the dog to the owner or family for a good fit. Just as it is silly for a young family with three children to purchase a two-seater sports car as its only means of transportation, a Great Dane living in a small apartment is equally impractical.

Breeds can often be categorized by size, activity, personality, haircoat, and other factors. A hyperactive, under-the-foot type of dog would not do well with an older couple that gets about with difficulty. Temperamental breeds may not fit in well with families that have considerable child traffic. High-care grooming breeds would not fit a busy life-style with no time for such grooming. It makes sense to start by identifying and selecting a breed or type of dog you can live with.

Remember, all dogs are different. If you learn to see and interact with each one as an individual with its own personality, you'll go far. If, on the other hand, you select a breed or type of dog and set out to buy the first available dog of that type or breed, you will have made a severe error in judgment. First, as I stated earlier, we can make generalizations about breed personalities, but you will also find the full spectrum of personality types among individuals within that breed. Therefore, after selecting a breed, carefully pick the individual pup with the desired personality characteristics you seek from that breed. Second, and equally important, select a responsible breeder from which to purchase your pup. What constitutes a responsible breeder is covered in great depth by the author, who has devoted an entire chapter to this topic. I heartily endorse her effort.

Regular grooming by the owner is very important and has great therapeutic ramifications for both the dog and the owner. This rubbing and touching creates a bond between dog and owner much like hugging does among family members. I see this not only in a long-term relationship, as with my own pets at home, but even on a short-term basis with pets hospitalized and cared for by my staff and me. Also, regular at-home grooming goes a long way in acting as a type of layman's physical exam employed by the owner, who can then have the opportunity to detect early warning signs of impending medical problems and thereby seek early treatment.

Attention to the actual training of a new pet dog is quite important as well. I equate training with just plain ol' good manners. Training not only involves formal public lessons, which are offered in most communities, but the manner in which we interact with our dog on a day-to-day basis. Remember, in every interaction we have with our pet we are either actively and intentionally or passively and unintentionally training and conditioning the pet on how to act and behave. A well-mannered dog gets to do more and be around people more because it is pleasant company. That's the origin of the old dog adage "An obedient dog is a happy dog."

Responsible Dog Ownership, my required reading for dog owners and potential dog owners, will benefit everyone. My hope is that it will help solve many behavior-management problems you may already be experiencing. More important, my desire is for this information to act as preventive medicine in the behavior-management department so problems may never arise. Believe me, it's no small wish or desire. Seventy-five percent of dog owners in America are afraid of their own dogs biting them! Pet overpopulation is soaring. Unwanted pets that never assimilated into the family are abandoned daily. Many medical problems seen by veterinarians are the results of poor management by owners due to lack of understanding or poor relationships with their dogs that could have been avoided with proper care. Not only does the dog suffer under these situations, but so does our society.

I know that this is a lot of information to consider concerning dog ownership, maybe much more than we have ever given thought to before. But it is a tremendous responsibility. Our loyal and trustworthy companion depends on us for everything, much like a child depends on Mom and Dad.

In our favor, there is great variety out there and a dog or breed for everyone. With care in selection and proper training, your new pet dog will fit perfectly into your lives for years of mutually rewarding fun and enjoyment. This is what I want you and Fido to experience.

My sincerest gratitude to Mrs. Davis for sharing her ideas and creating this remarkable book so that others may experience the treasures of loving and being loved by humankind's best friend.

DAVID JAMES NEWSOME, M.S., D.V.M.

Acknowledgments

To my husband, Bill, for all his support.

To my dogs, Saint, Angel, Star and Spirit, and to *all* dogs, for their love and forgiveness.

To all the people who helped with photographs for this book, including those we didn't have room to show you. I worked with obedience classes, dog groomers, veterinarians, responsible breeders, the city animal shelter, my neighbors, a police K-9 unit, participants at a sheep-dog trial, humane groups, assistance-dog trainers and others. My heartfelt thanks to all the dog lovers who gave so generously of their time to help spread the word about responsible dog ownership.

Regardless of whether your dog is big or small, old or young, purebred or "dawg," you are the source of its sustenance and happiness. This is the lifelong responsibility you agreed to when you got your dog. In return for the little your dog asks of you, isn't it only fair to do all you can to provide everything your precious dog needs as long as it lives? *Evelyn Shafer*

Preface

WHEN I was about sixteen years old, my actions cost a dog her life in a way I can scarcely bear to remember. I had a Chihuahua named Beau I frequently took for walks. On this day as I set out with Beau on leash, the family dog, a Dachshund mix named Penny, pushed open the latch of the chain-link gate with her nose and followed. I could have canceled my walk or put Penny in the garage, but with childish irritation I chose to ignore her and continue the walk. Unbelievably I even crossed a busy street with Beau, knowing Penny was still following and we were several blocks from home.

Cars along that stretch of road came rapidly around a curve that blocked their view of the way ahead. When I heard the jingle of dog tags followed by the squeal of brakes as a car made an emergency stop, I knew. Without stopping to look, I turned and ran back to where a kind motorist knelt over Penny, who had been killed instantly.

In most things I was a responsible kid, but the life of a dog is a lot of responsibility for a teenager. Young people are not completely aware of consequences, or of the finality of death. This incident could have killed even a human, occurring as it did in traffic. Penny paid with her life for me to learn a hard lesson.

People are not born knowing how to be responsible dog owners. We all have to learn. Proper care of a dog is expensive, time-consuming and *complex*. There are certainly no more unselfish and emotionally generous creatures than dogs. They give us all that they are. In the process they comfort, protect, help perform essential tasks, and even forgive us for sometimes unspeakable abuse. It is often through our thoughtless or uninformed neglect that we cause them to suffer.

I remember both painful and pleasurable steps along the path to becoming a responsible dog owner—and because there are always ways to improve, that journey has not ended for me. It's easy to forget, and sometimes we want to forget, what it was like not to know how to manage dogs properly—and what it must have been like for the dogs. But those of us who have learned must not forget that journey. We must understand and help every dog owner who asks how to solve the problems discussed in this book.

The questions I'm asked by all kinds of people whenever the subject of dogs is broached (and that's often, since I'm a volunteer therapy dog handler, working dogs in public frequently) have convinced me of some things. First, most people don't know enough about dogs to manage one. People don't know what owning dogs involves, but get them anyway. Eventually, they get rid of them. So many dogs come back, animal shelters might as well have revolving doors. Many dogs are born into this world only to be discarded. The cost to humans is extremely high in money as well as in the damage of becoming desensitized to the suffering of others. The full extent of the suffering endured by dogs is probably beyond our comprehension.

Second, it's probably too easy to acquire a dog. Maybe there should be a test, or at least a registration requirement, as for a license to drive a car or a permit to carry a gun. Maybe the requirements should grow more difficult according to how large a dog the person wants to own. Most people do not know that the responsibility of dog ownership is greater when the dog is larger, more protective, more aggressive toward other dogs, trained to use its teeth against humans or otherwise an increased risk to people.

Third, dogs are so important to people and provide so many benefits that it is worth the effort to solve the problems. There are solutions. Our basic education should include principles of responsible dog ownership.

Finally, people can learn. Communities are finding solutions in ways most of us who were concerned with this problem ten years ago never would have expected. Low-cost neutering is now available to all dog owners in many communities, when some years ago everyone said it was impossible. Dog training classes are moving beyond straight competition training and beyond techniques of the past that were sometimes overly rough and sometimes applicable only to certain types of dogs, so that now there is humane training help for all owners with all kinds of dogs, and dog owners are making these classes successful. Humane groups, training groups and responsible breeders are working together for the first time in many cases and are finding solutions that none could manage alone. Dog lovers are cooperating, and the impossible is beginning to happen.

Solving the problems of irresponsible dog ownership takes information, time and a willingness to acknowledge mistakes and to change. It's painful to admit we have reason to feel guilty and to get past the guilt to a better way, but it is also healing. In the process of making us better people, dogs serve us yet again.

Some of the models for *Responsible Dog Ownership* relaxing between photo shoots: these dogs would not be this calm if they really did live constantly in such severely crowded conditions. While these dogs really don't live this way, too many do, creating a sad state of affairs for companion animals in our society.

Note to Readers

Some of the photographs in this book are dramatic. Be assured that no dog or human was abused or endangered. We used trained dogs, skillful human supervision and creativity to tell the necessary stories with pictures. Photographs are the work of the author except where otherwise noted.

Please forgive the use of ''it'' when referring to a dog of unspecified gender. Every dog is unique and, whether neutered or not, is distinctly male or female. The English language just doesn't currently have enough pronouns.

Duke the Great Dane is eighteen months old and weighs 130 pounds. Penny the Maltese weighs less than 6 pounds. Dogs, at adult weights, range from the size of a premature human baby to the size of a large man. You can choose exactly the right size dog for your needs and capabilities. A dog is approximately as strong as a human three times that dog's weight.

1

Selecting a Dog
You Can Handle

RESPONSIBLE dog ownership begins before acquiring a dog, with careful research to find the right dog for you. People often choose dogs with less care than they take in selecting automobiles, yet dog ownership is a much greater responsibility. A dog's normal life span is from ten to fifteen years. Unlike a car, a dog feels pain, loneliness and fear as well as love, loyalty and a desire for companionship. However, just like they shop for an automobile, an alarming number of people select dogs based on appearance, dogs they formerly owned, or dogs met at friends' homes or dog shows. It's easy to see why so many cute puppies eventually become homeless adults.

This book is dedicated to helping dogs stay in their homes and helping owners form happy, responsible relationships with their dogs. This chapter will discuss basics to consider before making a choice, and the rest of the book will deal in more detail with the myriad duties of dog ownership. If you do not yet have a dog, reading the entire book before you get one will enable you to make an informed decision. If you already have a dog, this book concerns the daily decisions dog owners must make and will help you make good ones.

1.1 SIZE

The size of your dog is much more than a matter of personal taste and the amount of dog food you'll be buying. Perhaps the first consideration is whether or not you will be able to physically control the dog. If the dog is heavier than approximately one third your weight, you and the dog will need special training for control. You will probably not be able to physically restrain the dog without it. Giant breeds tend to be more docile than smaller dogs, but you can't count on that when, for example, the dog becomes highly excited.

While some extra-large dogs live indoors, many end up relegated to the outdoors because the owners did not realize how much they would shed, drool or otherwise alter home life. Often the size of the dog is the most decisive factor in how much time it will be able to spend with you.

The tiniest dogs are perfect companions for many people, even those who previously found fault with "yappy" little dogs or thought toy-size dogs were not "real dogs." However, if you already have a large dog or a young child or for some other reason need a sturdier canine, there are many dogs in the small- and medium-size categories to choose from. If your need is for a companion animal, life may be much easier with one of the smaller breeds. Be assured that each dog comes with a full-size heart to love its owner.

Interestingly, the best working dogs tend to be medium- to large-, not giant-size. Dogs in this range are likely to have more stamina and fewer genetic problems such as hip dysplasia to interfere with their careers. Be aware that if you do not have substantial work for a dog to do, most working dogs will seek out their own employment, possibly tearing up your property. The larger the dog, the more it can destroy!

1.2 ACTIVITY LEVEL

The breed does indicate how active a dog to expect, but even dogs born into the same litter can have different activity levels. The activity level will have a profound effect on mischief and damage to property. Also, some people find dogs with high activity levels irritating. A highly active dog is hard to ignore when you might prefer to be doing something else. My husband sends the dogs to me when they begin to annoy him! They seldom annoy me: I enjoy the company.

2

Herding dogs such as this Border Collie have high activity levels that allow them to perform the demanding work for which they were orginally bred.

Small dogs like Angel, the American Eskimo, can get enough exercise chasing toys indoors.

Would you like a dog to follow you around and exhibit a keen interest in everything you do, or would you sometimes prefer to be left alone?

If the dog will be alone a substantial part of the time or has an extremely high activity level, you may have to provide it with daily hard exercise. A small dog can get this exercise chasing a ball in the house, but an owner must work considerably harder—and get out in all kinds of weather—to exercise a large, highly active dog. However, if you work at home you may be able to keep the dog busy for enough hours of the day that hard exercise all in one burst is less necessary. It is also possible that two or three dogs living in the same household will exercise one another. Read the chapter about owning multiple dogs before planning on that solution!

1.3 PROTECTION ATTITUDE

A large percentage of dogs are selected because the owner wants protection. That is certainly uppermost in my mind when considering a new dog. However, I want a dog with enough, but not too much, protection instinct.

It's a sad situation when a dog chosen to protect the family ends up biting a meter reader or a child in the backyard. And what good does a protection dog do in the backyard when it is the house and the people in it that need protecting? A dog of any size in the house is more protection than the best-qualified protection dog that is not on the scene when needed.

If you are a police officer, or for some other reason have the task of apprehending criminals, you may need a heavy-duty protection breed and the training it takes for both handler and dog to do the job. If you are not responsible for catching the bad guys, consider a dog that will merely discourage them from bothering you in the first place and will chase them off if they persist. A dark-colored dog, especially if it has erect ears, will discourage many people who might mean you harm without having to lift a paw. A medium-size dog may be quite sufficient for the job. Success requires striking a balance between the dog you can manage and the dog needed to do the job. The dog will be more liability than protection if you do not learn to handle it.

Think carefully before giving your dog any training to bite. Once the dog has been taught that it's okay to bite human beings, you will have the responsibility of keeping it in training to come off the bite for

This police officer is an expert K-9 handler. Handling a large, protection-trained dog safely requires training and regular practice for dog and handler, as well as physical fitness. Training for control, without bite work, is more appropriate for most companion dogs and their owners.

the rest of its life. You will also have greater responsibilities in confining the dog, and your liability might be greater if the dog ever injured anyone. Even a burglar can sue you if bitten by your dog! Better to have your dog repel intruders without injuring them.

1.4 AGGRESSIVENESS TOWARD OTHER DOGS

Sometimes people think they want their dogs to protect them from other dogs. This can be a tragic error. If you plan to use your dog as a walking companion, you will discover that stray dogs are more likely to attack your dog than they are to attack you. This puts you in the middle and at greater risk from stray dogs. So, if you are afraid of dogs and want protection from them, a dog of your own is not the answer.

Many people are injured when dogs fight with other dogs, a trait that has no useful function in modern society. In the wild, canines fight to establish territory and to distribute the population to fit the food supply. They do not fight to the death. Humans have perverted this normal instinct to create dogs that will mindlessly kill each other as a human diversion. This abnormal behavior can be bred out of former fighting breeds, and has been by many conscientious breeders.

If your dog injures another dog, you are liable, and in some localities the incident would cause your dog to be classified as a dangerous dog. Dogs that desire to fight with other dogs without reason can be controlled through training and conscientious handling. If you are willing to accept this responsibility and are a capable handler, you can have a happy life with such a dog. It will limit, however, what other dogs you can acquire as long as you own that dog, the manner in which you can house your dogs, some of the activities you might have enjoyed with a dog that was easier to control around other dogs, and many other things about your life-style. Of course, the larger the dog with this trait, the more serious the owner's responsibility.

1.5 CONFINEMENT FACILITIES NEEDED

Even in rural areas, the days when a responsible owner allowed any dog to run loose are past. Many things will determine the facilities required to confine a dog, which will be discussed in detail in a later chapter. This can be the largest expense of all in owning a dog,

When dogs display aggression toward other dogs, people are frequently injured. Before selecting a breed or an individual dog, check out its attitude toward other dogs and make sure you can handle it.

Every time your dog goes outdoors it should be held on-leash or confined to a secure, fenced enclosure. Your dog's need to use the outdoors will be part of your life-style for as long as the dog is with you.

especially if you include the property some dogs destroy! It's best to either choose your dog to match the confinement facilities you already have or to upgrade your facilities before bringing the dog home. Some dogs can jump over any fence. Others can chew through any fence. Then there are the tunnel-diggers. If you confine your dog outdoors, will neighbors have to listen to it bark? That violates noise laws in many communities, and in all communities the barking disturbs neighbors.

1.6 GROOMING

Grooming is another subject that deserves a whole chapter, so be sure to check out that chapter later in the book before committing yourself to a dog! Grooming shops are full of dogs whose owners did not even know they would require professional grooming before they acquired them. Other owners vastly underestimated the cost and effort that would be involved. Worst of all is the tremendous suffering of dogs whose grooming is neglected. The answer to most of this suffering is not to acquire a dog you can't keep well-groomed throughout its life. There are many breeds that require little grooming, and they are just as lovable as the most elaborately coated dogs. What counts is that the owner's ability to provide grooming will match the dog's need for it.

1.7 TRAINING

Training is a part of dog ownership. The time spent to train a dog is also time the dog needs with you to fill its social needs. Most people lack the expertise for training and need the help of an instructor, either in private lessons or in a class. This instruction should start soon after acquiring the dog, no matter what its age. If you cannot locate an appropriate class, you will need to study books and other sources and educate yourself so that you can train your dog. However, dog training is a set of *skills*, not just a body of knowledge. It requires proper practice. A good instructor often makes the difference between success and failure, and that can determine whether or not you will be able to keep your dog.

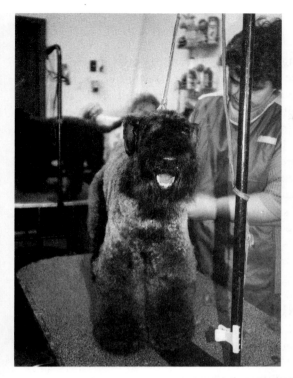

The Kerry Blue Terrier requires lifelong, regular, expert grooming, even if it never enters a dog show.

Karen and her Dachshund Emma have trained together and qualified on the therapy version of the Canine Good Citizen Test. Small dogs and their owners benefit from training, and when a dog can be carried in one's arms it is certainly easier to control.

The chapter on training will discuss in more detail the differences in dogs concerning the owner's training responsibilities. Dogs with protection attitude need more training for control, as do dogs with a desire to fight with other dogs. Larger dogs and more active dogs require more training. For some "easy" dogs, several weeks of a good puppy class may be enough, with perhaps a refresher or more advanced course after the dog passes puberty. Other dogs should be owned only by accomplished trainers and kept in practice on control skills throughout their lives. Thoroughly research the breed or breeds you are considering, and decide how much of a dog trainer you really want to be—before going out to look at cute little puppies!

1.8 POTENTIAL GENETIC ILLNESSES

Much of a dog's behavior is inherited, and so is much of its health. In both areas good care is necessary to bring out the dog's potential, and poor care will ruin both the behavior and the health of even a dog that has the best genetic heritage.

A tragically flawed temperament is certainly a genetic illness, since it can render a dog so shy that it is doomed to a life of misery or so aggressive that it cannot be controlled. A knowledgeable breeder can diagnose these problems when testing a puppy, and this is the kind of breeder you want to deal with—more about that in the chapter on responsible breeding.

What cannot always be detected are the many genetic health time bombs ticking in puppies, waiting to go off after their new owners have grown to love them. The dog may be condemned to a life of pain or an early death and the owner to tremendous emotional suffering and financial strain trying to care for the flawed dog.

Puppy buyers have no way of knowing enough about the genetics of the breed to determine whether or not their new family member is likely to be carrying one of these life-changing explosive devices. You can research the breed to find out what genetic problems have appeared. If you know what questions to ask, you may spare yourself much grief, provided the breeder is honest. Talk to more than one breeder. Assure yourself that the breeder you choose can be trusted with your heart and your checkbook.

Large dogs like Duke require more training for control than small dogs. Training is also essential for dogs with protection instinct and those inclined to fight with other dogs. Since you'll have to train, too, find out how much training you will need to select the right dog for you.

1.9 THE YEARS AHEAD IN YOUR LIFE

Are you a high school or college student? Are you planning to have a baby in the next several years? Is an elderly parent about to move in with you or into a nursing home where you will supervise care? What about your job—is a promotion that will mean working twelve-hour days in your future? All of these changes can influence coping with the responsibilities of dog ownership. None would necessarily mean you should not have a dog, but the dog needs to be chosen and trained for these future changes.

There are times when people feel restless in their lives and look for things to satisfy them. Many of the choices made at such times are thrown aside later. It's not fair to use a dog in this manner. So consider carefully your reasons for wanting a dog and the life changes ahead for you. Adopt a puppy only when you can reasonably expect to provide a home for the puppy for the rest of its life.

It has been well documented that dog ownership has health benefits for people, and a properly chosen dog can actually extend the life of an older owner. However, the wrong dog can cause its owner to fall, which is extremely dangerous as human bones get older. Additionally, a dog the person cannot handle will be a burden, not a benefit. Don't get a huge, aggressive dog to ''protect'' an older person who cannot control that dog! Besides harming family members and other innocent people, such a dog could actually prevent emergency help from reaching the elderly owner.

Sometimes a cat, bird or other pet is a better choice for a frail person than a dog: each case must be considered individually. If the person really wants a dog, consider a dog past puppyhood and with some training, a dog so desirable that the relatives would almost fight over who was to get it if the owner could no longer take care of it! Sending the dog to an animal shelter or to be euthanized when the elderly owner has to go into a residential care facility is unbelievably devastating to the person.

1.10 OTHER MEMBERS OF YOUR HOUSEHOLD, CHILDREN

If you live alone and can be reasonably sure your life will stay that way, you may need to satisfy only your needs in selecting a dog. If there are other people in your household, they must be considered.

This young puppy will be as large as the dog on the left in less than a year. Dogs are beneficial to children, but dogs are not toys. To avoid a tragedy in your family, never leave a child alone with a dog until the child is at least seven years old.

Brianna, Rachel and Danielle perform the important task of making sure their mom's dogs love children. Many responsible breeders and dog owners need to "borrow" children for this purpose. This practice can also give children from "dogless" households the benefits of relating to a dog without owning one.

Everyone in the home affects the dog's environment and the behavior it will develop. It's not enough to say that you will give the dog all its care and training. What if you are ill or take a trip and your spouse must take care of the dog while you cannot? What if your dog becomes ill and the treatment costs hundreds of dollars? What if the dog causes an injury and you are sued? What if the dog barks all night? Your spouse is committed when you acquire a dog, so the only way to be fair to your spouse and to the dog is to make it a joint decision.

What about a dog for the kids? If your only reason for acquiring a dog is because you think it would benefit your children, you don't really want a dog. Instead, provide your children with positive dog contacts through other means. You might be able to, with your children, assist a breeder or trainer in socializing dogs. This could even include occasionally having a dog come to your house to visit for an afternoon, a weekend or even a couple of weeks. You could also dog-sit for a traveling friend, neighbor or relative. If your child and family are up to the responsibility, you might take on the project of raising a puppy for a year, to be trained later to guide a blind person or assist a person with some other disability. Your children can receive good exposure to dogs in many ways without owning one.

Some parents mistakenly believe a dog can baby-sit the children when the parents are not around. Some dogs can safely be left alone with children who are past about age seven, but many cannot. Until a child is about that age, no dog should be alone with the child. If you wish to own a dog when you also have children, choose the dog carefully for the safety of both children and dog. A dog that is too tiny may bite if a child is allowed to frighten or hurt it. A dog that is large or boisterous may knock children down and injure them. A dog playing with children in the backyard may bite their friends or others who lean over the fence or enter the yard, mistakenly thinking they are threatening the family children.

In addition, many families are just too busy to take proper care of dogs. Acquiring a dog in such a case will cause the dog to suffer and will teach the children the wrong things about responsible dog ownership. If the adults in the household do not wish to own a dog for their own purposes, getting a dog for the children will do the children more harm than good.

By now you know that selecting a dog is not a simple matter. If dog ownership sounds right for you, read on. There are hundreds of breeds of dogs and many ways to adapt your facilities. The dog can learn to adapt to some extent, too. For people able to keep the necessary commitments, responsible dog ownership is a satisfying life-style with many benefits.

To undertake responsible dog breeding, one undertakes the stewardship for both life and death—they are not mutually exclusive. As soul satisfying as dog breeding can be, it has numerous pitfalls and should be conducted only by those who are motivated by the desire to breed only to maintain and refine the breeds. Magnificent animals like this Great Pyrenees group never happen by chance.

2

Responsible Breeding

WHETHER seeking a puppy for yourself, considering becoming a breeder, or deciding the politics of dog breeding, you are concerned with what it takes to be a responsible breeder. Irresponsible breeding causes unspeakable suffering in dogs, inflicts emotional and financial stress on owners, and burdens society with the expense of huge numbers of dogs for which there are no homes. This has led some well-meaning people to decide there should be no dog breeding at all. These people are not aware that responsible dog breeders do exist, although they are in the minority. Rather than stop all breeding, we should support the efforts of those who breed responsibly and penalize those who do not (preferably to the extent where they will stop breeding dogs and leave it to those who will do it properly).

2.1 HEALTHY DAM AND SIRE

Responsible breeding demands that the dam and sire—mother and father—of the puppies be healthy. Unfortunately, it is common practice to breed dogs that are in questionable health, sometimes from ignorance but usually because it's expensive to keep breeding dogs in proper health.

To generalize that any breeder who produces more than a certain number of puppies a year is irresponsible would be inaccurate. However, the volume of puppies is certainly a factor to consider. No female dog should produce a litter of puppies on every cycle. If this is the breeder's practice, the mother dog's health is in jeopardy.

Some conditions that pose hazards to the puppies cannot be safely treated once the mother-to-be is pregnant, so a responsible breeder will do the necessary health checks beforehand and will consistently keep all dogs on the premises in excellent condition—a healthy dog is built from the inside out, and not in a short time. It takes a lifelong commitment from the breeder.

While potential puppy buyers are often advised to see both the dam and sire before selecting a puppy, this is not always feasible. The best breeders do not breed to the male they happen to own if there is a better male available. Breeders who purchase one male and one female and breed the two of them regularly to one another may not be doing the best for the puppies genetically. Using only healthy dogs to produce puppies means making the hard decision to eliminate a dog from breeding at any time there is a problem with that dog's health that could negatively affect its puppies.

When male and female do not live on the same premises, it is customary to send the female to visit the male's home, since they are less likely to fight there. Breeders make all sorts of arrangements in order to provide proper care for puppies and good lives for the adult dogs used for breeding. Sometimes the mother dog lives in a home with a family, visits the breeder once or twice in her life to have puppies, then returns to family living. This also discourages the use of one dog over and over. While careful breeding to tight genetic lines can improve qualities in a breed, excessive use of one dog can lead to tragedy when it is discovered later in that dog's life that it passed a previously undetected genetic defect to many of its offspring. It is better for the overall genetic health and strength of any breed to breed a larger number of well-qualified individual dogs a few times each than to use one dog many times, however outstanding that dog might be.

You should also question the health of the dogs when a kennel breeds dogs of several different breeds. There are outstanding kennels that handle two or three breeds, but a kennel that produces puppies of several breeds is more likely to be inferior.

18

This female dog (left) is in heat, and the male dog is more than willing to father her puppies. But he, though an excellent dog, is not the breeder's choice as the best possible stud in this case.

2.2   GENETIC KNOWLEDGE OF THE BREED

One reason to watch out for a kennel that produces puppies from several breeds is that the breeder is likely to lack genetic knowledge of all those breeds. Such a breeder may be producing puppies as livestock, with no detailed knowledge of genetics. The best breeders make a lifelong study of this subject for one or at most a few breeds and leave a lasting legacy of better dogs and knowledge to the breeders who follow them. Such breeders may own or co-own quite a few dogs and control the genetic decisions, whether or not those dogs all live on the breeder's premises. If you desire to become a breeder, you would do well to apprentice yourself to such a person, rather than strike out on your own and perhaps cause many dogs to suffer.

The genetics of any breed is both science and art. Your happiness as a dog owner may well depend on the knowledge and ethics of the breeder who produced your pet. Unless you do years of intense research, you cannot know what a responsible breeder should know about the genetics behind your puppy. On this matter more than any other, you are at the breeder's mercy. Before acquiring a puppy from any breeder, be sure that you totally trust this person. Many matters that affect your future happiness with the dog are solely in the hands of the breeder.

2.3   TEMPERAMENT, TRAINABILITY
AND SUITABILITY AS PETS

Behavior problems kill more dogs than genetic illnesses do. This can be a real gray area because the breeder may claim—and may honestly believe—that the dog's owner caused the problem by poor handling. And sometimes this is the case. A breeder who maintains contact with puppy owners throughout the lives of the dogs has a much better chance of becoming aware of genetic temperament problems because the problems will occur in a variety of homes with puppies from similar breedings. A responsible breeder will place temperament equal in importance to other factors such as health when planning matings.

Temperament is a highly variable quality, with no one best or perfect temperament for all dogs, for all breeds, or for all owners. For example, dogs that will be exhibited in the show ring need some "sass

Conformation dog shows help breeders select the right combinations of dogs for breeding. The way the dog moves, its coat, its temperament and other qualities are all considered in order to earn a championship. Other events, such as herding and hunting tests, help select dogs for working ability. Responsible breeders work hard to determine which dogs to breed.

This puppy demonstrates a natural instinct to retrieve. Knowledgeable breeders can use a variety of tests to evaluate puppies accurately and place each in a home where it and the new owner will be happy with each other.

and brass'' and will preferably be placed with knowledgeable dog owners who enjoy living with high-powered dogs. A dog may have only moments to show the judge its stuff, and the easygoing temperament you might prefer for your family companion dog could be a disadvantage in the show ring.

There are many variables in a dog's temperament, yielding an infinite variety of actual temperaments: in other words, dogs are just as different from each other as people are. To make things more complicated, temperament is profoundly influenced by the environment the dog lives in and the handling it receives. Unfortunately, few dog owners are knowledgeable, skillful and committed enough to shape some of the more difficult temperaments into well-adjusted ones. That does not necessarily mean all those dogs have ''bad'' temperaments. It means that a huge percentage of dogs are placed in the wrong homes, homes where those dogs are likely to fail but other dogs would have succeeded. This is partly the fault of people who acquire dogs casually, and partly the fault of breeders, who should know their dogs, accurately temperament-test their puppies and match them with the correct owners. A breeder who offers you the ''pick'' of the litter for a pet is probably behind the times. A breeder should be knowledgeable enough to place puppies in the proper homes, according to each puppy's conformation and temperament and the time the breeder spends getting to know potential puppy owners.

Trainability goes hand in hand with temperament, but it is possible that training is not what you plan for your dog. Since people learn and grow in their ability to train dogs, this area causes a lot of confusion. The worst problem is that people see a trained dog working with a handler and go out and buy a dog of that breed for themselves, without knowing what it takes to turn a *trainable* dog into a *trained* one. They also do not realize that a trained dog will only be able to use its training with a skilled handler—and the handler is not included when you buy the dog!

The most trainable breeds can often be the worst problem dogs when living in homes with owners who do not train. Dog training is a life-style with your dog and a whole way of relating to the dog. Some people have what seems to be natural ability, which may stem from childhood experiences with dogs. But most people require skilled instruction from a qualified dog trainer. The breeds and individual dogs that will be right for you depend heavily on your preferences concerning training. If you do not wish to train with your dog, you might be quite

If you choose a dog of one of the highly intelligent, very trainable breeds, be sure to work with your dog to give it all it needs. Too many such dogs end their days in pounds because they went to owners who should never have had them.

happy with a dog that is not very trainable. Such a dog can be far less of a problem, when placed in a well-matched home, than a potential Rin-Tin-Tin is when placed with an owner who doesn't train.

Even dogs thought to be untrained usually have some training, however, if their adjustment to their homes is satisfactory, and it is essential that your dog be capable of the training it will need. This might include house training, walking on a leash politely, learning how to behave with guests, and perhaps many other behaviors. Before acquiring a dog, decide on the essential behaviors for your dog and discuss this frankly with the breeder. A responsible breeder should make every effort to match you with a dog of the proper potential, whether that be smooth family life or dazzling skill in some area outside the home. The trainability is only potential, however. Properly training the dog is the owner's responsibility. If ever a breeder advises you that his or her breed will not suit your needs, that is a breeder that puts the welfare of the dogs before profit. Be grateful for such advice.

2.4 THE PROFIT MOTIVE

The desire to make money leads to many abuses in dog breeding. Only a small percentage of responsible breeders profit financially, and these few are at the top of their profession due to well-deserved reputations for placing quality dogs. In other cases where people profit from breeding dogs, it is at the expense of the dogs and their prospective owners. Such breeders need to be put out of business. You can help by never paying money to such a person, no matter how sorry you may feel for the dogs in his or her power. That breeder will only use your money to cause more suffering.

The fact that a dog is ''AKC registered'' means that its dam and sire were registered and the American Kennel Club has not caught the breeder in any action warranting forfeiture of AKC registration privileges. A somewhat stronger indication of a quality breeder is membership in the national parent club for that breed. All AKC breeds and many other breeds have parent clubs. These organizations make decisions for the welfare of their breeds and usually have codes of ethics all members agree to follow.

When you pay a responsible breeder for a dog, you are not buying puppy flesh. You are compensating the breeder for all the services that have gone to produce that puppy—and for the future services you can

It is a common misconception that breeding purebred dogs is an easy, lucrative pursuit. Actually, it is neither easy nor lucrative. Every breeding, every litter and every puppy represent enormous amounts of effort on the part of the breeder. The primary concern is breeding good dogs, keeping some to breed and show and seeing the others in loving, happy, responsible homes.

expect from the breeder as you live with your dog. Good breeders put far more into their dogs and puppies than you could ever pay them. If you are considering becoming a breeder yourself, you should know that you are unlikely to earn a profit. For worthy dog breeders, it is an expensive hobby. The breeder who places the welfare of the dogs over any potential profit is the one who deserves your support.

2.5 WAITING ARMS

One obstacle to profit in dog breeding is the limited number of suitable homes. A responsible breeder will not produce dogs without a reasonable expectation of placing them in good homes. Those few top breeders whose dogs are highly sought after may be able to sell all the puppies they can produce, all to carefully selected homes. But most breeders will have to limit breedings according to the available owners. Puppies should be produced only when there are "waiting arms" for them, homes where they will be cared for properly, valued and loved. Many problems will be solved when the day comes that all puppies born into this world have homes waiting for them.

2.6 PLACING PUPPIES FIRSTHAND, NOT THROUGH A THIRD PARTY

A responsible breeder will personally interview prospective owners and place puppies. Co-ownerships can involve other parties with responsibility or authority to place puppies, but you don't want a puppy that was bred in one place and passed to another for sale. This results in many problems for the puppy and the new owner.

The proper care of a young puppy includes keeping it in a clean environment, since even careful vaccinations and the best of care can leave young puppies vulnerable to contagious diseases. Puppies need to go directly from their breeder's home to the homes of their new owners. Until its vaccination series is complete, a puppy should not be exposed to other puppies outside its breeder's kennel.

Puppies also need contact with littermates in order to develop properly, and should not be removed from their mothers too early. To assess temperament, the breeder needs to raise the puppies to the proper

Responsible breeders produce puppies only when there are enough homes for them all. These puppies will always have homes, because their breeder will see to it.

A responsible breeder will want to know you and will want regular reports on the dog throughout its life.

age and observe them in specific situations, including interaction with littermates. One puppy temperament test can reveal some information, but the best testing is done more than once and includes breeder observations during puppy development.

Responsible breeders match their puppies to compatible owners by getting to know the prospective puppy owners. The breeder wants to know if you will give the dog a good home and if your home is the right one for that particular puppy. You want to know if you can trust the breeder that this puppy is healthy through and through. The relationship between breeder and owner can be maintained by mail and telephone, but not by a third party selling the puppies so that breeder and owner never know each other.

A young puppy that is not placed directly from the home of its breeder is at high risk of catching a contagious disease and may be physically or emotionally handicapped for the rest of its life if it survives. Oddly, third-party sales are often priced much higher than you would pay when dealing directly with a responsible breeder. The best puppies are only available directly from their breeders.

2.7 CARE OF THE PUPPIES

Conscientious breeders put in long hours of difficult work to insure the health of each litter of puppies. Until they are in their new homes the puppies keep the breeder busy, and the novice might well be shocked at the work involved. If you are considering raising a litter of puppies, find an expert breeder of the same breed to serve as a resource all along the way. Ideally this person should be someone worthy of the status of mentor. It is an excellent idea for new breeders to begin by co-owning with such breeders and relying on their judgments when breeding and their reputations when placing the puppies.

2.8 SOCIALIZATION

Puppies need a surprising amount of socialization while living with their breeders, and the longer the puppies stay, the greater this responsibility becomes. A breeder sometimes keeps a puppy longer because its temperament is uncertain and it needs more observation or

Keeping a litter of puppies healthy involves diligent maintenance of cleanliness. Puppies raised in dirty conditions are likely to have worms, skin problems and difficulty later with housebreaking.

Young puppies eat frequently, day in and day out, whatever the weather or other demands on a breeder's time.

Dogs and puppies depend on their owners for clean, fresh water. They spill it and play in it, and it can become too hot or can freeze, depending on the weather. When deprived of potable water, dogs can rapidly dehydrate or die.

Puppies require an enriched environment to stimulate their minds and bodies so they will grow into healthy, intelligent adults. Here a puppy discovers that it can reach the food dish by climbing the ramp. Throughout life, this dog will be more comfortable and confident walking on uneven and unusual surfaces than it would have been without this experience.

Purebred dogs are commonly found in animal shelters along with mixed breeds. If you have a problem with your dog, contact the breeder. Deal only with a responsible breeder who can ensure that you will never have to leave your dog at an animal shelter should you not be able to keep it.

because the pup's conformation looks likely for show. If the puppy is placed in a home after spending extra time in kennel life, the breeder's efforts at socialization will become critical in determining whether or not the older puppy or dog will be able to adjust to a new environment. Even before they are the minimum age to leave the litter, puppies need the correct handling and the correct experiences. This book will not attempt to describe all the social experiences necessary for puppies, but suffice it to say that a puppy needs to meet those things it will later live with and to do so by the proper age and in positive ways, or it will not be able to cope later.

2.9 PROVISION FOR DOGS THAT LOSE THEIR HOMES

This is a tough requirement that needs to be met by every breeder worthy of being called responsible. If a breeder produces a puppy and that puppy ever again needs a home after the breeder has sold it or given it away, that puppy or dog—at whatever age—is the breeder's responsibility. That does not mean the breeder has to give people their money back because they have decided they do not want their dog anymore. There are conditions that call for refunds, such as a dog with a genetic defect or a dog that turns out differently than promised. How a breeder handles the money end of these issues is also a measure of responsibility. But the bottom line is the breeder's willingness to take the dog back, no matter what the circumstances, if the owner cannot or does not want to keep it anymore, and to either find the dog another home or provide a home for the rest of its life.

This is a tough requirement to place on breeders, but the responsible ones accept it gladly. Some go a step further and are willing to take any dog of their breed that is in need. Breeders who will accept back their own puppies are usually the same breeders whose dogs are in demand and who have waiting arms for the dogs they produce. Since these breeders are a small minority, many people—in reaction to the endless flood of homeless dogs that have to die due to irresponsible breeding—do not believe they exist. But responsible breeders do exist, and they deserve the support of all those who love dogs. These breeders do not cause the problem of homeless dogs: they are part of the solution.

This is a partial view of the lobby of an animal shelter. People giving up their dogs place them behind these doors.

The numbered doors from the animal shelter lobby open into these cages. When a dog finds itself here, it is never the dog's fault. Every quality of a dog is due to human involvement in the breeding, training and handling of that dog. Yet the experience of an animal shelter is, for a dog, much like prison is for a person. Humans cause this suffering, and only humans can change it.

3

Neutering

3.1 POPULATION CONSIDERATIONS

Many people feel that the only reason to spay or neuter their dogs is to help control the overpopulation of dogs. The problem with this belief is that it leads to misconceptions.

One of these misconceptions is that, since we have such a tragic overpopulation of dogs that causes the suffering of animals and expense and danger to humans, we should stop all breeding of dogs until the problem is solved. I hope the chapter on responsible breeding has helped you to understand that this is not the solution. Responsible breeders do not contribute to the dog overpopulation problem. Instead, they provide those who want puppies with a responsible alternative, and at the same time they are the main hope for the genetic health of future dogs.

However, it is true that only those who wish to join the small group of truly responsible breeders, and do all the things necessary to insure that their puppies never contribute to the problem of unwanted dogs in any way, should breed dogs. In order to stop the problem of homeless dogs, we need to work to see that every puppy born into the world has a breeder standing beside it for its entire lifetime.

The idea that the only reason to neuter your dog is because of the overpopulation of dogs leads to a second misconception: people think that their dogs will never get out and therefore will not contribute to the problem. They often feel that, much as they would like to help a good cause, they cannot financially afford to do so. Of course those who feel their dogs will never contribute to the birth of unwanted puppies are often wrong! Later in this chapter we will discuss many other reasons to neuter your dog.

But what about this overpopulation problem? If there aren't lots of stray dogs dropped off near your home, or if you have not thoroughly investigated your local animal shelter, you may not realize just how serious it is and what an awful price dogs and people are paying.

The figures change every year and vary according to community, but the reason homeless dogs are suffering by the millions is irresponsible dog ownership. Most homeless dogs are produced by people who assume no responsibility at all for them once they have been sold or given away. When an owner decides to get rid of a dog, it is either left out to fend for itself—the absolute worst thing to do—or given to the first person who will take it or dropped off at the nearest animal shelter.

Who pays for this expensive problem? Part of the expense is covered by fines on those dog owners who can be identified as irresponsible, part by license fees from responsible dog owners (irresponsible owners avoid licensing their dogs) and the rest by taxes.

Some people profit from the excess of dogs that makes homeless strays inexpensive to procure. Homeless dogs are often used in scientific research, some of which benefits humankind but some of which is repetitive and done only to secure research grant money. People who train dogs for fighting sometimes take homeless dogs and let the fighting dogs kill them for practice. Owners who would be horrified to know the fate of their pets may well be dooming them to terrible deaths by just not caring enough.

That care begins by making sure you acquire a dog you can handle. A huge percentage of homeless dogs are young adults acquired as puppies by people who were not prepared to cope with the adult dogs they would become. As you will discover later in this chapter, neutering the dog is an important step in coping.

3.2 ADOPTING FROM AN ANIMAL SHELTER

If you decide to adopt your dog from an animal shelter, avoid adopting a puppy. The exception to this might be when, for some

Today, it is possible to acquire almost any kind of dog you want at an animal shelter, the reason being so many of these unlucky animals were first acquired by people who should have researched to find the right kind of dog for them and just didn't bother. They also weren't there later to see the suffering they caused.

unusual reason, both parents are known. In that case, the same considerations would exist as when selecting any puppy. But this is rare. Generally a puppy in an animal shelter is either on its own or with a mother dog. In a few cases the puppies are actually purebred. If you wish to consider a purebred puppy or dog from an animal shelter, find a reputable breeder of the breed involved to help evaluate the dog. These people have knowledge of their individual breeds that is beyond the comprehension of most of us.

The best choice from an animal shelter is an adult dog. If you do not know enough about breeds and temperament to evaluate the dog properly, find someone to help you who does know. Many knowledgeable dog people volunteer their time to deal with the tragedies of homeless dogs and are happy to help a dog find a good home. Such a happy ending can make the rest of their work easier to bear. If the dog is a mixed breed, remember that every breed that contributed to it must be considered. Also, if a certain breed is not right for you, you should avoid any mix containing that breed.

When exact parentage is unknown, mixed-breed dogs are often the best health risks, since there is a good chance that any genetic health problems from purebred ancestors will be counteracted by other genes in the mix. It is common, though, for mixes to inherit the most extreme behaviors from both sides! Many dogs are left at animal shelters because they are too active for their owners. Sometimes this is because they are working-type dogs, whether mixed or purebred, who were living with owners who did not train or work with them. What those owners considered bad behavior may be exactly what an owner who trains and works his or her dog is seeking. Professionals who train drug-detection dogs and dogs for people who have disabilities frequently find in animal shelters perfectly good dogs that have been discarded by their former owners.

The most accurate temperament testing of a puppy depends upon knowledge of the breed and the ancestors of that particular pup. The size of a puppy when grown and the type of grooming that will be required also depend upon knowing the dog's ancestry. These things can be evaluated without guessing when you adopt an adult dog.

It is hard to describe how stressful it is for a dog to go through a shelter where dogs must be euthanized due to overpopulation. Dogs were not intended to be together in such large groups, and sometimes the housing combines dogs in such a way that some of them are terrified. With their keen senses, all of them are aware that dogs are

This Boxer was adopted through a Boxer club rescue organization as a result of our trip to the animal shelter to take pictures. He was carefully evaluated by people who know the breed, given veterinary care and placed with an experienced Boxer owner. Many breed clubs have such rescue groups that can help when individual breeders fail. These groups are excellent sources of potentially great adoptive pets.

This Dachshund, whose former owner died, is going home with a new owner thanks to the efforts of a humane rescue organization that cares for dogs in foster homes until carefully selected new homes can be found.

dying in that place. Dogs adopted from an animal shelter where dogs are put to death have been under terrible stress and may suffer ill effects for some time afterward. This is another reason not to adopt a puppy from such a place. Their immune systems are immature and they often die later from illnesses they were exposed to in the shelter. It's seldom the fault of the shelter, but of the situation forced on them by the huge numbers of homeless dogs they must handle with limited resources. An adult dog has a much better chance of surviving the experience. It will probably have a lasting effect on the dog's temperament, but if what you want is a dog that will love you and try to please you, the dog may have these feelings all the more for having gone through its time of horror at the shelter.

Animal shelters want to see as many of the dogs placed in homes as possible—they grieve for the dogs they have to kill. The public does not wish to think about the consequences of irresponsible dog ownership and the dogs that have to die as a result. It is time to stop tucking this horror away out of sight. School children need to learn about this problem right along with such issues as conservation and saving the environment.

If you desire a dog of a particular breed and want to do your best to combat the problem of unwanted dogs, a reputable breeder of that breed should be able to help you get on the list for a rescued dog. Many breed organizations, as well as individual breeders, give some of their resources to taking in dogs of their breed that are homeless. Some will go to animal shelters and bail them out, while others may only be able to help the dogs they themselves produced that need second homes.

If a purebred dog in this situation is of unknown parentage, the responsible breed rescuer will make sure it is neutered before being placed, since no one could predict what genetic problems it might be able to pass on. This person will also be able to evaluate the dog's temperament and much of its physical condition, due to his or her special knowledge of the breed. The breeder will also be able to evaluate *you*, to help you decide whether or not a dog of this breed is right for you.

Many people say they could not visit an animal shelter because it would be too upsetting. Yet many of the same people are contributing to the problem! Education may not change those who truly don't care or who profit in some way from activities that produce homeless dogs. But if you really love dogs, you will do your part to solve this problem.

Here's how: Let your dog bear or father puppies only if you will take on all the responsibilities involved for the rest of the lives of those puppies. Adopt a dog only when you are 100 percent committed to responsible dog ownership. Neuter any dog that is not part of a responsible breeding program as soon as your veterinarian says the dog is ready for the surgery. Teach—by example as well as in words—those around you what it takes to be a responsible dog owner. Once the people who are causing problems due to lack of knowledge are converted to responsible behavior, the force of law will be much better able to deal with deliberate offenders. In the darkness caused by the ignorance of the vast majority of dog owners, dogs are suffering and dying.

3.3   A PUPPY TO KEEP

Many entire litters are bred in order to yield one puppy for the breeder to keep. If your dog came from a reputable breeder who will supervise your breeding and has homes for the rest of the puppies and hopes of producing one or more superior animals, breeding to produce one standout might be a reasonable thing to do. Usually this does not work well. It would be far better to go back to the breeder or to some other breeder who works with your breed of choice and obtain a healthy puppy that has been expertly bred. You might be happy with a rescue dog that is no longer a puppy. There are so many dogs available, no matter what your preferences or financial resources, that producing a litter to get one pet puppy makes no sense. And because of the stress and danger to the mother dog, it can have tragic results.

3.4   "NATURAL" BREEDING BEHAVIOR

Most people realize what is happening when they see a male dog mount a female dog, but that's about the extent of common knowledge about breeding behavior in dogs. Responsible breeders supervise matings, because either partner can be injured. An event called a tie normally occurs, in which the two dogs cannot pull apart. This can cause panic in an inexperienced dog, and the ensuing struggle can result in injury. When a large male mates with a small female, as often happens with dogs their owners have not neutered, she can be injured.

This is what can happen to one of the puppies you placed from your litter because you needed one "just like Trixie." Surrendered to an animal shelter, this Cocker's once-beautiful coat is now filthy and matted and his chance of finding a happy home extremely small.

Four Bichon Frise puppies would be three too many if you had bred your dog just to get one puppy. What would happen to the other three?

I used to have neighbors who allowed their two mixed breeds to mate, and the female, about one third the size of the male, would scream. A couple of months later she would have another litter of unwanted puppies.

Many owners of unspayed female dogs are not aware when their dogs are in heat. I often know when one of my neighbors' female dogs is in heat before the owners know. My male dog, Saint, may sniff the fence, sniff the urine left by the female dogs he lives with (both spayed), and sniff his females hopefully. He may show some mounting behavior with them, which is easily discouraged since he was neutered at around one year of age. I may also see strange dogs around, attracted by the scent of the female in heat. And the female involved is likely to exhibit some unusual behavior, such as making more noise than usual or getting out of the fence.

A female dog can be impregnated only when she is in heat, and some owners feel they can prevent that from happening by taking special precautions during that time. But that will only work if you know when it is! Some females do not show signs, and when they do, more often the owners don't pay enough attention to notice them. The female is attractive to all male dogs when she is in heat, even some that have been neutered, and may be powerless to protect herself from dogs that are stronger than she is. In effect, she is vulnerable to rape.

Among wolves, which are the best example we have to determine what would be natural canine mating behavior, mating cycles occur once a year. In dogs they occur twice a year in most breeds, due to centuries of breeders selecting the most fertile dogs for breeding so that they could produce more puppies.

Wolves have a social order within the pack that regulates mating. Only the dominant pair mates. The other wolves in the pack are not allowed to mate, and in years when food is too scarce, not even the dominant pair mates. The entire pack contributes to the survival of a litter. Wolves do not always eat what they have hunted right where it falls, but often carry chunks of food and bury them in caches to eat later. They can carry food for mother and young by overeating and returning to the den to regurgitate for the others to eat. Many of our pet dogs also have the ability to regurgitate at will. My dog Angel was suffering from severe malnutrition when adopted from an animal shelter at age eighteen months, and she exhibited behavior related to the wolf. She would accept food whether she was hungry or not. If not hungry, she would try to hide the food for later. Sometimes she would take the

The caring breeder never leaves a dog alone in a run with a bitch in season to achieve a mating. These Belgian Tervurens are in the initial stages of the mating act and their handlers are right there if human intervention becomes required.

fresh food and attempt to bury it in the house by pawing blankets aside and putting the food under them. Other times she "wolfed" down the food and, on a trip outside to relieve herself, dug a hole and regurgitated into it, then covered the predigested food over with dirt. If I watched her carefully, I would see her return to eat it later. This was sad to see, revealing what a difficult time she must have had as a young dog. It shows how powerful these instincts can be.

The breeding behavior of dogs—with females going into heat twice a year, males always ready to mate with any female in heat they encounter, and little or no social structure involved—is *not* natural behavior. The idea that letting a dog mate is better because it is more natural is incorrect. Natural breeding behavior in dogs is rare.

Much harm is caused by the stupid jokes on television and in movies concerning the mating and neutering of dogs. The idea that a male dog is angered by being neutered is nonsense. Sex does not mean to dogs what it means to people. Dogs are companions to humans, genetically selected throughout recorded history for that purpose. Depriving a dog of human companionship is what makes it unhappy, not depriving it of a sexual drive that often causes it problems. Many dogs can enjoy social relationships with other dogs, part of their common heritage with the wolf. These relationships are smoother, safer and more feasible for dog owners to provide when all the dogs involved are neutered. Humankind created the unnatural breeding habits of dogs through long-term selective breeding. It is our responsibility to deal with it in the way that is best for the dogs. Dogs are highly domesticated animals that cannot survive in the wild. To allow them to mate because people think it is more natural for them is to behave irresponsibly out of a sad lack of knowledge.

3.5 YOUR DOG'S HEALTH

I once knew a business owner who had a tiny poodle he carried with him to work, a precious pet he adored. His children were all grown and the charming dog brought him much pleasure. One day he decided to breed her because he was sure her puppies would be wonderful. Having the puppies caused her death.

While some dogs have puppies easily, some cannot bear puppies without surgery. Even a veterinarian can't always predict the likely complications with a particular female. If you love your dog very much and she is very precious to you, have her spayed so that her life is not at risk through having puppies.

Some people still believe the myth that a female dog will develop a better temperament after having a litter of puppies. This can be tragically untrue. Some females become aggressive and dangerously unmanageable and even have to be put to sleep for the safety of humans after having a litter of puppies. If the female dog has a temperament that is less than desirable, she should *not* be bred, because it is likely that some of her puppies will have temperament problems worse than hers.

Your female dog's best chances of avoiding breast cancer in later life are by being spayed before her first heat. Unspayed female dogs are susceptible to other cancers as well, more so if they have had puppies. Responsible breeders frequently have female dogs spayed after their breeding years are over, unless they plan to continue showing them in events which do not allow neutered dogs.

As male dogs age, those who have not been neutered will probably suffer from prostate trouble, and those who have been neutered at a young age will probably not. There are exceptions, but this problem is common in intact male dogs and neutering at a young age usually prevents it. Neutering not only protects against prostate enlargement but also against prostate cancer, a significant killer of dogs.

It is almost certain that your dog of either sex will be healthier if you have it neutered, and these health benefits increase with age. Cancer associated with the reproductive organs is common in dogs, and neutering, among its many other benefits, largely prevents these cancers.

3.6 BEHAVIOR CONSIDERATIONS IN UNSPAYED FEMALES

If more people understood the behavioral differences brought about by spaying and neutering their dogs, I'm not sure the veterinarians would be able to handle all the surgeries! Unfortunately, some highly responsible breeders have a blind spot in this area, since their own life-styles require living with intact dogs. They have no opportunity to observe the wonderful behavioral benefits of this surgery. Breeders as well as veterinarians are often reluctant to recommend neutering as a specific solution to a problem an owner is having, because there

My three neutered dogs enjoy good health and lots of energy to help around the house!

Routine activities such as taking your dog for a pleasant walk have to be changed when she is in heat. Spaying eliminates this problem and fosters better health. One owner of a retired champion and Utility obedience dog declares that spaying made her dog act at least three years younger, almost immediately.

can be no guarantees. Once a dog has started a sex-related behavior, neutering may reduce the *drive*, but the *habit* may persist. Also, many behavior problems are partly due to sex drive and partly due to lack of proper training and management by the dog's owner.

However, neutering is one of the best aids to dog training that exists. Let's consider the behavioral benefits of neutering, first for the female dog, then for the male.

A female dog in heat can be a strange creature indeed! First, there are the coat changes. This is particularly true of breeds with long, fluffy hair. Some females lose their entire coats on every cycle. They can cycle every six months, every nine months, or even just once a year—you don't find out until the dog has established a pattern. Dogs in the same kennel tend to go into heat together. If for any reason you need your dog to look presentable at all times, this can be quite a problem. Spaying the female may cause one more coat dumping, but after that she will experience only seasonal changes, which are much less drastic. A female who "blows" coat due to cycling or to having a litter of puppies can lose it all, starting with the entire coat turning completely dull and falling out over a period of weeks. A full and fluffy coat can easily take four months to grow back, and longer to reach its full potential.

Therefore, the female who cycles twice a year can be out of coat *most* of the time! By contrast, seasonal changes in spayed females occur once a year, with sometimes a lighter shedding period at another point in the year, and the coat that falls out is mostly undercoat, leaving the shiny guard hairs. Undercoat has special qualities, including the ability to grow back rapidly. The coat can be full about two months after a seasonal shed. This is one reason why in some breeds the male dogs have a tremendous advantage over the females in conformation shows. Males, after the change from puppy to adult coat, shed mostly undercoat and quickly come back into the full coat that is such an advantage in the show ring. Females used for breeding have far less time during the year to look their best, and some never do until after they have been spayed.

Besides the coat, there are many other changes in a female dog because of her cycle. An owner may become familiar with a dog's patterns after getting to know her well, but there is always a degree of unpredictability. A trained dog that is used for some form of work may have personality changes during parts of the cycle, including the time before the heat when you are not exactly sure where she is in her cycle. She may become less reliable on her commands, or show odd temperament changes such as shyness.

Many owners who say their dogs do not exhibit these changes do not use the dogs for work, and therefore do not observe them closely. During a dog's heat there are behavior changes, too, including more frequent urination, which is part of attracting a male (whether that is what she really wants or not, it happens). For a time my neighbors allowed their female to use my front yard to relieve herself when in heat. Male dogs I had never seen before came around to investigate. One dog's owner wound up in court because his dog was in my front yard on the same day that a dog of that breed and color mauled a cat to death in the neighborhood. Irresponsible dog owners cause all sorts of problems for others.

If you need to take a female in heat out, you will encounter other inconveniences. During the time my Star was in heat before we had her spayed, we kept her on odor-masking tablets from the veterinarian to minimize the effect on male dogs. I could not continue my normal activities with her, such as taking her for walks, because it would have been foolish to risk encountering a stray male dog I might not have been able to handle alone. In the house she wore pants and pads to keep the discharge from staining furnishings, and this all had to be removed each time she went outside to relieve herself, a real nuisance. My dogs stay in the house, so confining Star was not a special problem. People who normally leave their female dogs out in the backyard all the time do have special problems with confinement, because the fence can suddenly not be enough to keep her in, or male dogs out.

Spaying your female dog does away with these ups and downs and allows you to get to know her better, to train her better and to work her more consistently. Even with a female whose cycles are fairly regular, all plans concerning activities with her are uncertain for a large part of the year. You don't know exactly when she will go out of coat, when she will be fertile or when she will be attractive to males. For a good two months at up to two different times of the year, you may have to be tentative about your plans.

3.7 BEHAVIOR CONSIDERATIONS
IN INTACT MALES

It is easy to see why the one thing people commonly know about male dogs is that when they are neutered they are less prone to wandering. Since some males are almost irresistibly drawn to the scent of a female in heat quite a distance away and will go through obstacles to get to her, neutering them before they ever mate with a female is a great prevention. If you wait until they have already established the behavior, neutering may only help a little. This is true for much of the male sex-related behavior, since hormones start the behavior but habits can keep it going. The smartest dog owners have their male dogs neutered by the time they are about a year old. This is also the most beneficial time healthwise. However, it is a good idea to have any male dog neutered at any age, provided he is fit for surgery. The benefits can't be guaranteed, but there are always some.

Fighting with other male dogs is also reduced by neutering, as is general aggressiveness. But the dog's genuine ability to protect is not harmed. A dog that is just generally aggressive is not the best protector, anyway. The best protection dog is the well-behaved dog that is *with* you. If you need serious protection, you and your dog should have special training. A trained dog that is neutered will respond to commands much better than one that is not neutered. Sheer viciousness is no asset in a personal protection dog.

I have read that neutered male dogs will not lift their legs to urinate, but that has not been my experience. It may have to do with the dog's exposure to other dogs, the age when it was neutered and other individual variables. It is less likely that a neutered male will lift his leg to mark his scent inside your house, but there's no guarantee he won't, especially if he is a tiny dog that considers the inside of your house a large area. A larger dog will be more interested in extending his territory outdoors by marking only there. A neutered male will be less obsessed with scent marking, especially if neutered at a young enough age. But if this would be a serious problem for you, you may wish to avoid owning a tiny male dog and have a female instead. If you already have this problem, get expert advice on managing your male dog and properly cleaning the marked areas in your home to remove urine scent so he won't be attracted to mark it again. All dogs are not created equal with regard to relieving themselves in the house, and there are breed as well as sex differences.

Many of the differences between neutered and intact male dogs are minimized in specific cases by highly trained intact males versus badly managed neutered males. A neutered male is easier to train and handle, if neutered at the right age, than the same dog would have been if not neutered. However, some dogs are easy to live with in the

A neutered male dog is no less protective of his home and family and may show better judgment in separating friend from foe. Saint guards the front of the house from inside through a window, where his threat display can warn intruders without dangerous, face-to-face confrontations.

Neutered males are less inclined to mark urine inside your house.

first place, and there is no way to be sure what a particular neutered dog would have been like in later life if not neutered. I got a glimpse of it, though, with my Saint a few months before surgery, which had to be delayed slightly until he recovered completely from demodectic mange. For a while I nicknamed him "Razorback Hog Puppy," because at any small excitement, such as someone on the other side of the fence, the hair on his back all the way from neck to tail would stand on end. It was excessive excitation, often accompanied by a smelly anal gland emission. Shortly after neutering surgery, the "Razorback" phenomenon disappeared. Since then extreme arousal can raise the hair at the base of his tail and neck, but never the whole length of his back, and anal gland emission seldom occurs.

For a brief time some years ago I sold Avon products. In one young lady's home I met a big, fun-loving dog named Moose that she said was three years old. I remember him during that brief visit as being on the move, happily playing with a toy. She told me her veterinarian had said that since he had been neutered, Moose would "always be a puppy." That was before I got Saint, but now that Saint is nearing twelve years of age I think it is also true of him. He's very open to making friends and playing to form new relationships, rather than squaring off to see who is more dominant. He loves to play with people, other dogs and toys, and attention to his diet has kept him slim and handsome. His health is terrific and he skillfully relates to people as a therapy dog. He continues to learn new things. When I had him neutered it was not common practice, and one assistant in the veterinarian's office tried to make me feel guilty by spitting out the word "castration." In technical circles that word is fine, but it has many human connotations that do not apply to dogs. I had Saint neutered because he was a dog of unknown ancestry and had no business reproducing, and because I thought it would be best for him. That turned out to be more true than I could possibly have known.

3.8   THE CAREER DOG

When I got Saint, I had planned a career for him as my walking companion and to make me feel secure at home so I could sleep and shower when my husband was away without feeling afraid. Since then Saint has performed those functions admirably, as well as two or three other careers. Most of us cannot know when we acquire dogs exactly what activities we might want to pursue with them through their long lifetimes. Yet to get maximum benefits a male dog needs to be neutered when young. There are a few careers for which male dogs cannot be neutered, such as breeding and some police jobs. For the dog to become a police dog you would have to give him up. Police departments typically use intact dogs, and males only. But in the future that may change.

For most careers, being neutered is an advantage to both male and female dogs. Imagine a dog assisting a disabled person if that dog had to be out of commission when in heat, three weeks at a time, twice a year. These female dogs are spayed and the males are neutered to minimize their distractibility when working. Neutered dogs are much steadier on their commands around other dogs.

Being your companion is a career for a dog. If you are to have maximum enjoyment of your dog as a companion, it needs to be neutered. Keeping it intact, even for legitimate breeding purposes, will give you less use and enjoyment of your dog than you could otherwise have had. This is one sacrifice that responsible breeders have to make.

3.9 WHAT'S BEST FOR THE BREED?

There are a few cases where breeders are needed to save a breed from extinction. I have often said that in such a case, and only then, I would be willing to accept the responsibility of breeding. However, this is not going to come about because you hear on the news that some breed is "rare" and puppies are selling for huge sums of money. By the time you hear that, the scarcity of a breed is over! In fact, it's highly likely that within a few years there will be many of that particular breed that were produced carelessly out of greed and will have the health and temperament problems to prove it. Seldom is a breed truly in need of breeders. Most breeds suffer from the opposite problem: far too many breeders.

So what's best for the breed, any breed? Do you love your dog enough to care about its whole family, all the dogs of its breed? Any purebred dog is fairly closely related to all the dogs of the same breed. Do you genuinely want what's best for the breed?

If so, base the decision about whether to breed or to neuter your dog on heart-to-heart talks with highly respected breeders. Your dog should pass all the health checks recommended for the breed, and to do that it will likely have to be at least two years old.

Your dog's welfare is more important than considerations of the breed as a whole. That includes your needs, since the dog's welfare depends partly on your needs being met. A breeder may feel that not being able to use your dog's genes would be a loss to his or her breeding program, but it is highly unlikely that the breed as a whole would suffer. Make an agreement with the breeder before you acquire the dog as to exactly what your obligations are concerning neutering, breeding and exhibiting the dog for titles. Do some soul-searching. Does a title mean a lot to you? Have you ever pursued this activity with a dog before? If not, you may find it different from what you expect. Other than an agreement to neuter the dog, don't make any commitments to a breeder unless you trust him or her with your dog's life, because that may be at stake in breeding. Some very ambiguous situations can arise, such as a health problem where your veterinarian recommends spaying your female dog for her own safety, but the breeder or co-owner demands that she be treated with medication instead, so she can still be bred. If both parties put the dog's welfare first, such problems will be more easily solved.

I used to feel guilty that I had my dog Star spayed before she could earn a championship, even though the breeder agreed. I simply could not live for long with an unspayed female dog, and she was dumping her coat twice a year, so earning a championship could have taken a long time. She has three champion littermates who have also distinguished themselves in performance events. Star has helped to spread the good word about therapy dog work and has provided thera- peutic benefits for many people. I did not enjoy conformation events and will not take that route again, but I'm proud of Star's canine family and her breeder is proud of Star. Producing puppies is not the only way to do what is best for the breed.

3.10   LIFELONG RESPONSIBILITIES

My Angel, besides malnutrition, demodectic mange and other health problems, was in heat when I adopted her from the shelter. She had been brought to the shelter along with a male of the same breed. Trying to trace the background later, I got the impression that she may

It would be difficult to schedule Star's therapy-dog visits to health-care facilities if we had to try to plan around the heat cycles of an unspayed female. A female dog in heat can be unpredictable in her behavior and can cause other dogs to misbehave and therefore is not worked in public during this time. Dogs in careers such as assisting people with disabilities are neutered in order to focus better on their jobs.

have been the result of a brother-sister mating, and I suspect that she had previously had puppies. Her horrible physical condition could have easily been caused by having puppies without proper care. She also had hookworms and coccidiosis, and her ears had dropped from the malnutrition. The ears came back up most of the way with two weeks of special food, including vitamins and baby food, and she gained weight rapidly.

I can't do anything about the puppies Angel may have had, except shake my head and feel sad. But had she had puppies after coming to me, they would have been my responsibility for the rest of their lives, if I were to do the right thing. I suppose Angel's previous owners took some responsibility when they gave those two little dogs the ''Christmas present'' of dropping them off at the shelter. I chose Angel to be my Christmas present that year, and due to her illness she was an expensive one!

When it became apparent that she was in heat my veterinarian decided to spay Angel right away. She was forming a wonderful relationship with neutered Saint, drawing tremendous confidence from him. Spaying her after the heat was over would have required keeping them apart for about a month, possibly damaging their new relationship irreparably. She came through the surgery well, healed quickly, and when the veterinarian took the stitches out he was able to release her to play freely with Saint again. They have now been pals for years and years. Even a neutered male can mate and tie with a female dog, one reason that neutering all of your dogs allows the safest and best relationships among them.

Dogs depend on humans for their very lives. Responsible breeders struggle endlessly with the problem of keeping their puppy-buyers from producing unwanted puppies. Such breeders care about those puppies, and their puppies, and their puppies' puppies. It is a responsible breeder's nightmare for a puppy he or she produced to wind up being used like a machine to produce puppies for profit with no concern for the welfare of the dogs involved. Neuter your dog. You'll be glad you did, and you'll have the right to brag!

4

Confinement

CONFINEMENT can represent one of the major expenses of dog ownership, and the expenses tend to take owners by surprise. When we acquired Saint, my husband and I agreed that he would stay outside in the backyard, which was already fenced. We expected no expenses at all related to confining him. But the reality was different.

First we realized that, due to the location of our property, leaving Saint outdoors would expose him to teasing and to danger from things tossed into the yard by thoughtless people passing through the parking lot next to the fence. We also realized he could escape the six-foot stockade fence (although he never did), and might well do so out of boredom. And his barking could anger neighbors.

Without really making a decision, we began by leaving Saint in the garage with newspapers while we were both away at work, letting him stay in the house with us when we were home and in the bedroom with the door shut when we went to sleep. Saint was a hyperactive nine-month-old dog when we adopted him from the animal shelter, and he dug a hole in the sheetrock in the garage to get to the fiberglass insulation, which he tore out and played with. That gave him a cough. We also installed an air-conditioner vent in the garage to protect him from the oppressive September heat. The confinement expenses had begun!

After about a month Saint stopped using his newspapers in the garage during the day, so we felt he was ready to stay in the house while we were gone and provide security against burglars. Then the real expenses began. Some of the more memorable damages were to carpet, walls, furniture and interesting things he found lying around. He nearly went back to the animal shelter the night before Thanksgiving when we returned home to find a sofa cushion disembowelled on the living-room floor. It was easily repaired, but at first sight the roomful of foam bits made my husband feel that Saint was absolutely tearing the house to pieces.

I can't give a dollar figure for all the damages, since most of them we patched or decided to live with, having our house decorated in ''early Saint'' until we gradually replaced things over the years. I figure it was several years before his burglary-prevention ability (his record there is 100 percent—no burglars wish to meet him face to face after seeing him through the window giving his standard warning!) caught up to his early house-wrecking. On that fateful evening we decided to stick with him, damages and all. That was a smart decision, and a happy one.

We could have put Saint into one room or a crate while we were away, but he would not have been able to fully protect the house. His wild chewing continued until age two and a half, which is not unusual for some breeds of large, active dogs, but many dogs drastically reduce destructive behavior by the age of one year. Now that all my dogs are well past those youthful forays on the house's interior and contents, I can be fairly confident of arriving home to things pretty much as I left them. But there will be a new young dog one of these days, and I'll strive for patience, creativity and commitment to deal with the inevitable nonsense.

Saint's checkered youth is described here not because it is such an amazing story, but because it is so normal and typical. Every dog owner has to decide how to confine the dog, and no one system is right for everyone. This chapter will explore the responsibilities dog owners have toward confining their dogs, and the choices.

4.1   WHAT CAN HAPPEN TO THE DOG?

Loose dogs are in grave danger and pose hazards and expenses to the community. Laws vary, but in any community a dog at large

Improperly confined dogs are frequently injured or killed in auto accidents.

found to be dangerous is at great risk of losing its life. If a dog is in the country chasing livestock, the livestock's owner may have the right to shoot the dog now and discuss the matter later. City or country, loose dogs can be hit by cars, hurt or killed by other dogs or people, lost or stolen, or confiscated and put to death by authorities. They are also frequently hurt or killed by neighbors who are fed up with their negligent owners.

Dog owners are easily lulled into complacency when a dog has been loose for a period of time and nothing has happened yet. They assume that nothing ever will. But many things can stimulate even a dog that seems completely incapable of getting excited, and no one, including the owner, can be absolutely sure what an unattended dog might do. Additionally, the dog does not consider a city lot to be the extent of its territory unless it is rather harshly trained to its boundaries. It is natural for a dog to spread its notion of territory to an ever-larger area, wandering farther and farther until it gets into trouble from which it cannot return. Dogs that wander don't last as long as dogs kept responsibly confined by their owners.

4.2 HOW ARE OTHERS AFFECTED?

Tragic as is the lot of the wandering dog, the effect on others is the bigger problem. The owner is liable for damages, but frequently cannot be identified, and does not even know how his or her negligence harms others. The harm can be devastating, and, sad to say, it affects responsible dog owners more than it does those who cause the problems.

Harm done by a wandering dog is never the dog's fault. Blaming the dogs has resulted in ineffective laws being passed that are unfair to responsible dog owners. It is not true that any particular breed of dog is innately bad and should be made extinct. Every breed has individual dogs with good temperaments and owners who are responsible. Those who try to solve community problems by blaming the dogs are choosing an approach based on ignorance of responsible dog ownership. Confinement is part of that responsibility.

In spite of romantic notions about a dog's thought processes and behavior that people pick up from silly movies and television programs, no dog is sufficiently aware of all the factors involved to be held responsible for escaping its own confinement. If the dog *can* get out,

How did this unlucky dog end up in an animal shelter? Keep your pet in secure confinement to avoid having this happen to him or her.

the confinement is not adequate. If the dog got out today, the owner's responsibility is to solve the problem before tonight! That may involve securing the dog temporarily in the house or on a tie-out (tying a dog out regularly can severely damage its temperament, so this should be only a short-term measure) or sending the dog to a boarding facility until sufficiently secure permanent arrangements can be made. It does not mean doing nothing until the dog gets out again, or until it is convenient. Dog ownership is not always convenient when owners are responsible. It's never boring, either!

Why is it so vital to act immediately at the first sign that a dog can and will escape its confinement? Here is a partial list of how other people suffer when a dog runs loose:

1. Their property is fouled by the loose dog's waste. This spreads disease, especially hookworms and other intestinal parasites. Other pets and even children can be infected. The property owner also faces dealing with the mess. If not picked up, it can foul the blades of mowers and tractors. Urine can damage plants.

2. Loose dogs can spread fleas and ticks onto lawns and shrubs where they wander. These parasites can then infest other dogs and people who use the same area.

3. Loose dogs can attack other animals, creating hazards for those who wish to walk with their own dogs on leash. These can be horrible experiences, resulting in injury to owners and injuries or death to leashed dogs. This is traumatic to the victims, and many never get over it. Humans may forever fear dogs, and dogs that survive an attack can become permanently fearful or aggressive toward other dogs. The owner of the loose dog may not even know his or her dog is capable of such behavior—and a dog that would not have done it last week may become territorial enough or excited enough to do it this week.

4. Loose dogs can attack people, especially young children who can appear like prey. Older children who run from these dogs or otherwise behave inappropriately, in a dog's frame of reference, can be at risk. When someone is killed by a dog, it is usually a very young child. Others attacked by dogs may carry the scars for life. Rarely do such events occur the first time a dog shows dangerous behavior; but when people do not

Chasing a child can begin as a game for a loose dog but can quickly escalate into something much worse. Even if the dog is only playing, the child can be terrified or hurt—even killed.

understand dogs well enough to detect dangerous behavior, tragedies can happen.

5. Loose dogs can cause automobile accidents. They also cause related damage, such as when a driver swerves to avoid a dog and hits something else. The dog's owner is liable for all damages, if he or she can be identified.

6. Loose dogs deprive other people of the use and enjoyment of their property. This can include many types of behavior, such as damaging plants and menacing people so that they do not feel free to come and go as they please.

7. Loose dogs cause other dogs and owners to suffer through mistaken identity. More than one dog has been put to death because a serious misdeed was committed by some other dog and the wrong dog was accused and punished. The more responsible you are, the more easily you can fall prey to this, because neighbors know you have a dog that looks like the perpetrator. Make sure that you develop a reputation for being so responsible that people may testify on your behalf if such an accusation is ever made.

8. Loose dogs cause responsible dog owners to suffer through the passing of more restrictive laws.

4.3 LANDLORDS

If you rent your home, you may have to discuss with your landlord arrangements concerning the confinement of your dog. Some landlords are very uninformed about dog ownership and place impossible restrictions on their tenants. Your sincere efforts as a responsible dog owner may help you persuade your landlord to adopt a workable arrangement.

If you live in housing that shares a wall with another resident, the noise your dog might make must be carefully considered from the beginning. Is there a way to prevent your dog's barking from disturbing your neighbors? This can drive the most dog-loving neighbors absolutely berserk over time, through lack of sleep and the feeling of the loss of control over their own home environment. The stress from a neighbor's barking dog is cumulative, and training may not solve the problem. It works in some cases, but not in all, and requires great dedication from the owner if it is to work.

If you are planning to go out, you might be able to confine the dog to a crate in a room which is far enough away to prevent the barking from carrying through the wall. You might be able to have the dog surgically debarked, although this surgery is controversial. If done by an expert, it is preferable to getting rid of the dog, which so often ultimately results in a homeless dog that is put to death.

Don't wait for anyone to complain about your dog's barking. As soon as you find out this is happening, solve the problem and let the neighbors know you have done so. If you don't think your dog is disturbing others, keep lines of communication open with all your neighbors, and ask them regularly if there is a problem. People are very reluctant to complain to dog owners. Some will come to you only after they reach the breaking point, creating a potentially dangerous encounter and a neighbor who will be difficult or impossible to satisfy. Others will not speak to you at all, but will go straight to authorities. If you leave neighbors in the difficult position of having to bring up the subject, you may not hear about the problem until it is too late to satisfy them.

Countless dogs become homeless when tenants keep dogs without permission in situations where landlords have the right to evict tenants or make them get rid of their dogs. In order to have some security for your dog, get written permission before moving a dog into the property.

A good reference from a former landlord of an apartment where you lived with the same dog you currently own may serve to persuade a landlord to rent to you. You may also be able to come to a reasonable agreement about how you will confine the dog, such as the use of a crate whenever you are not home. When your circumstances change, have another discussion with the landlord—or landlady, as the case may be.

These issues are difficult for both sides. Unless you qualify under laws that guarantee a tenant's right to own a dog, finding a place that will allow it depends on how desperate property owners are to find tenants. In a renter's market, where lots of properties are vacant due to not enough renters to go around, landlords are more willing to take a chance on whether or not you and your dog will cause problems. These problems can force landlords to deal with noise, complaints from other tenants, devastating property damage and even involvement with dog bites. In a market where there are enough tenants for all the properties available, landlords often ban dogs to spare themselves the hassles.

4.4 DAMAGE EXPENSES

Why are landlords so concerned about the damage a dog might do? Unlike a homeowner, who like me might decide to just live for a while in a house decorated in "early Saint," a rental-property owner faces having to restore the property before it can be rented to another tenant.

Some years ago I worked for an agency that checked leasing applications for prospective tenants. The single most important part of the application was former landlords. I would call, long distance if necessary, and obtain specifics of former landlord-tenant relationships. Those that upset me most were people who had moved away and left dogs abandoned on the property. Fortunately I encountered few of those. But what I often discovered were tenants who had left owing hundreds of dollars in damages, sometimes caused by pets. This could include fleas, uncleaned waste matter, torn carpeting and furnishings and other damage. Overly excited dogs have been known to break windows and jump right through them—and turn around and do it again after the windows are repaired.

In my own experience as a tenant, I once spent some unpleasant weeks sharing a wall with a tenant who left two large dogs alone in the townhouse apartment for long periods. The noise was unbearable, but I never complained to the management because it was so bad that I knew it would not be tolerated for long. However, I was not prepared for the damage I saw after the tenant moved out and the management sent crews in to make repairs. Laid out on the unit's front lawn were huge pieces of wrecked carpeting and one interior door that had been completely penetrated by clawing. The fault was not with the two sweet dogs, but with an irresponsible owner. Such incidents make it more difficult for dog owners who need to rent a place to live.

The least a tenant can do is to meet his or her legal responsibility and pay damages. But in my job checking tenant applications, I learned that many do not. That makes it easy for me to see the landlord's point of view, much as I sympathize with dog owners.

Whatever decisions you make about how to confine your dog can result in unexpected expenses for damage. Dogs in the house can tear up things you would never think possible. Dogs in backyards can destroy fencing, garden equipment, expensive plants and even the exterior of the house. Saint came to live with us just before we signed up for cable television, which had recently come to our city. My

A young dog found the knobs on this sofa a tempting target and an outlet for unsanctioned chewing.

This chair was at just the right height for a teething puppy to "antique."

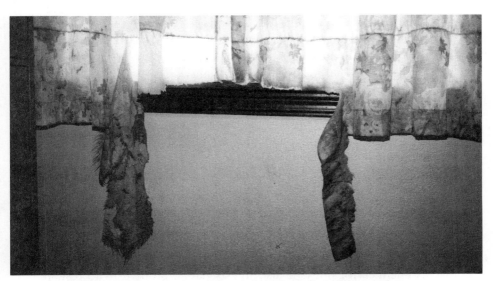

A dog's jumping up to see out the window can easily destroy your drapes.

65

husband was home with Saint the day it was installed. After the installer had gone, Bill sat down to watch television for a moment while Saint was outdoors. As he watched, the newly installed cable began to disappear into the wall! He checked outdoors and found Saint pulling it.

A creative dog owner, Bill loaded Saint into the car and drove to a hardware store. There he found a long piece of galvanized metal he could use to protect the outdoor part of the cable. He put it into the car and started home. On the way the wind caught the part of it that was sticking out the car window. It made a terrible noise and frightened Saint, who then had a foul-smelling anal gland emission and tried to crawl under the brake and accelerator pedals. Imagine the damage if Bill had lost control of the car. Fortunately, he did not, and the version of the story he told me when I arrived home that day was rather tame, designed to reassure me and keep me from nagging him! Over the years he has mentioned more and more of the details. I took the metal off the outside cable connection last year, but I didn't throw it away. Who knows what the next young dog to join our family will try?!

4.5 FREE RUNNING

Some otherwise responsible dog owners follow a practice called free running their dogs. This is advocated by many dog trainers. I have no doubt that it can increase a dog's confidence, give it the opportunity to form healthy social relationships with other dogs, and help dissipate energy that can otherwise be a problem indoors. Sounds great, doesn't it? The problem is, it is often at the expense of other dog owners and people in the area. The owner of the free-running dog may be watching the dog, but if the dog is a hundred yards or so away, a lot of things can happen that the owner does not see. A free-running dog that is not under reliable command control makes matters worse, but command control does not always solve the problems that this practice causes.

One problem is that owners do not walk that hundred yards or so to pick up their dog's waste. It is so easy for the owner to rationalize that it's a big, "wild" area, and perfectly "natural" to leave the waste. But the truth is that there is *no* area we should spoil in this way and it makes enemies for dogs. It also infests public property with disease and intestinal parasites.

It is not uncommon for large dogs, left alone and bored, to chew holes in walls.

See the free-running dog's handler in the distance, wearing a white coat? Even a friendly dog can annoy, traumatize and injure other people when running loose to play. Even a trained dog may fail to obey when overexcited in a play or chase attitude.

Another problem is dog fights. When a dog is running free it is a threat to other dogs in the area, including those walking on leashes. The free-running dog may be friendly toward the dog on the leash and try to play with it. The dog on leash may feel threatened or may be a type born with a desire to fight with other dogs. This puts the owner of the leashed dog in the middle of a nightmare, while the free-running dog's owner, at a distance, may never fully realize what he or she has caused. It's not the dog's fault—the finer points of human law and courtesy are beyond a dog's thinking ability. That's the owner's job.

And what about the effect of free-running dogs on people who are afraid of dogs, or allergic to them? How can the owner tell that the dog, 100 yards away, is not frightening someone or causing them to become ill? This practice just creates yet more people who will fear—and hate—dogs.

The time has come for dog owners who wish to free-run their dogs to band together and create fenced areas that, either all the time or during specific posted times, will be dedicated to dog running. The dog owners need to arrange regular clean-up of dog waste. There is simply no other responsible way to carry out this activity, in spite of the fact that it is a common practice with many owners who strive to be responsible.

4.6 OFF-LEASH TRAINING

Working a trained dog off-leash on commands the dog will reliably obey and under full handler attention is not free running and can be an appropriate off-leash activity in a suitable place. This is completely different from free running a dog, since in this case the dog is working and is under control. Some communities allow this legally, and others simply look the other way as long as dog and handler are obviously trained and create no problems. Many dogs that will not reliably come to a handler when called from free running 100 yards away are totally reliable when called from a steady stay position 100 *feet* away.

The potential danger with working a dog off-leash on commands is that the dog may not be as reliable as the owner thinks it is. Part of the problem is the handler who is not sufficiently skilled to give the dog his or her attention the entire time the dog is off-leash. If the dog is reliable it may be appropriate to work it on commands in the front yard. But no matter how reliable the dog is, it is not appropriate to leave it off-leash while the owner turns his or her attention to conversation with a neighbor who strolls by. Always have a leash with you when working your dog, and put it on the minute you wish to turn your attention elsewhere.

What does it take to bring a dog to the point where off-leash work might be appropriate? The breed of the dog is a major consideration. Some dogs were bred for work that cannot be done on-leash, such as retrieving and herding, and with diligent training and good handlers they can learn to work off-leash with a high degree of reliability. Other dogs will never be reliable off-leash, but this doesn't mean they can't be great companions. If an owner considers a leash a terrible inconvenience, chances are good that he or she has not had sufficient instruction and practice with the leash. Owners need to gain this skill in order to enjoy dogs in public.

After years of practice, a leash feels to me like an extension of my arm, a natural part of me. You can become comfortable with it, too, and your dog can learn that the leash means freedom, not restriction. A dog on leash can go out in public and enjoy the sights and smells. A trained dog on leash, given permission, can relax its attention on the handler and enjoy the walk.

Training for off-leash work begins by training on-leash and taking the leash off to work only in confined areas. When the dog is reliable, try working on-leash in public areas to find out if your dog reacts differently than at home or in obedience class. Most dogs will react differently when they first encounter distractions, otherwise known as "temptations"! While making the transition to off-leash work, the handler uses a long line to work the dog at a distance without letting it off the leash. A convenient form of long line is the retracting lead, which comes in various lengths. These leads are wonderful, too, for handlers whose dogs are well trained but have breed propensities that make them unsuited for off-leash work in public.

After the dog works flawlessly on a long line and is completely steady off-leash in a confined area with distractions, it may be reasonable to try commands off-leash in public. Approach this cautiously, and remain ready to put the leash back on at the first sign the dog is unreliable. It is the exceptional dog and owner who can handle off-leash work.

Even a reliable team can make many enemies by working in the wrong place at the wrong time and offending people who do not know that handler and dog can be trusted. If someone is hurt, the handler

Sheepdogs of all breeds have been bred to respond well to off-lead control and to possess the character trait of responsiveness to the owner's wishes even when off-leash—*if* properly trained and working with a skilled handler. These abilities are necessary for herding work.

Police K-9 dogs use their training and responsibility to perform some of their work off-lead. This dog is on guard while his handler searches the "suspect" in a practice session. In a real arrest, the dog's ability to work off-lead frequently safeguards the lives of police officers. A police dog bites only when suspects resist and represents much less danger than a gun—the well-trained police dog can be called off while a bullet cannot. Modern police dogs are seldom killed in the line of duty, and usually retire to private life when their working days are over.

Star's passive nature, training and genetic propensities combine to make her a good candidate for off-leash work. If your dog is not this steady or might be too quick to chase passersby, add the safety of a long line or retracting lead when working outside a fence.

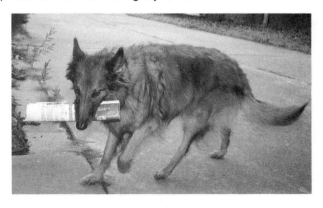

will be liable for damages and the dog at risk of being put to death, even if it was legal in that location for a trained dog to work off-leash. A mistake indicates that either the dog or handler was *not* trained well enough to work off-leash. Dogs have to work off-leash to do certain jobs, but only when on command and trained to the degree that the command and the focused attention of handler and dog are as strong as a leash.

4.7 BREED DIFFERENCES CONCERNING CONFINEMENT

Just as some breeds can work off-leash on command and under handler attention reliably and others cannot (although individual dogs exist in every breed that are great workers), owners have different responsibilities concerning confinement, depending on the breed and the individual nature of the dog.

Some dogs are more inclined to bark than others, increasing the risk of unhappy neighbors, unless the dog can be kept in confinement that muffles the noise. Even inside a free-standing house, the owner or others in the house might find a noisy dog intolerable. The owner could later decide to keep the dog outdoors, creating a problem for neighbors who have to hear the noise. Training sometimes helps, but it's best not to adopt a vocal dog if noise would be a problem. There are quiet dogs, and then there are dogs that find it so difficult to be quiet that teaching them can border on cruelty. It's more humane to start with a quiet dog if that's what you will need.

Owners frequently receive unpleasant surprises when they plan to keep their dogs outside in fenced backyards. Trespassing children, meter readers, and others who have legal access to backyards and who are hurt by the dog can cause a disaster for the owner and death for the dog. Some breeds are much more likely to try to protect property and get the owner in trouble than other breeds are.

Some dogs will stay in backyards and others will not. My neighbors had a Siberian Husky who repeatedly left the fenced yard until they finally stopped looking for her. Yet another neighbor has an Alaskan Malamute in a yard with a fence of the same short height who has been perfectly content for years to watch the world go by, commenting on it occasionally with her beautiful howl, without ever trying to leave the fenced area. Why does one dog of a breed that was

Some dogs can chew right through chain-link fencing.

Wood fences can lose slats, sections can fall down, portions can decay—one icy morning a car slid into my fence and knocked a hole in it that even my large dog could have stood up straight and walked through! Any fence used to confine a dog needs constant inspection.

born to run prove true to its heritage and take off repeatedly, while another stays happily at home? The Malamute's owners pay a lot of attention to her, allow her to go in and out of the garage at will through a dog door, and handle her intelligently. She was also spayed at a young age.

4.8 BACKYARD

So what about keeping a dog loose in a fenced backyard? How good a plan is this? Not so good, usually. Most of the time the backyard dog suffers from the "out of sight, out of mind" syndrome. Without much attention, the dog becomes dirty and unkempt and isn't welcome in the house. It also becomes overeager to greet humans after a long time alone, and no one wants to interact with a dirty dog that jumps on them.

Many backyard dogs leave the yards, sometimes without the owners knowing it, although after a few times the owners may begin to suspect and may choose to do nothing about it. It is easy to consider the outdoor animal as something less than a member of the family. It is easy to forget or ignore how much trouble the situation is causing for others. It is easy to blame the dog.

Meter readers and utility service people have much trouble with backyard dogs, and these relationships tend to deteriorate rather than improve. The dog tends to become more and more aggressive as month after month the intruder, from the dog's point of view, comes into the yard and leaves when the dog threatens. Meter readers have to cover ground quickly, leaving little time to befriend dogs. They also take vacations and change jobs from time to time, leaving backyard dogs to deal with new meter readers. Sadly, some meter readers resort to violence, and one whack with a club can damage a dog irreparably. It can also turn a dog that was formerly undecided about meter readers into a real attacker. Then it is only a matter of time until a disaster occurs, which often means a bad end for the dog and a large financial judgment against the owner. Utility companies and other service providers such as the post office have attorneys and are skilled at taking dog owners to court. The owner is not likely to win. He or she can expect to pay for medical care and the worker's time lost from the job. Dog bites can put people into the hospital and keep them out of work for weeks. Few of us can afford such an expense, and even if homeowner's

The backyard dog frequently finds a way to escape, spurred by boredom. Responsible dog owners keep their dogs safely confined, using methods which can vary according to the dog.

Star doesn't need a bed of her own, since she shares ours. For the safety of all humans in your home, do not allow a dog on a person's bed until it will get "Off the bed!" *immediately* on command.

insurance pays for it, the dog owner's policy may be canceled afterward.

Many dogs cannot endure activities on the other side of the fence, and children often tease backyard dogs, usually in ignorance. This can turn a dog into a dangerous animal, and even if the dog does not leave the yard but bites someone who is hanging over the fence or trespassing, the owner can be held liable. The law is not usually on the side of the dog owner.

Providing food and water for a dog outdoors can be complicated. If water is spilled or placed in the sun in the summertime, the dog can fall victim to heat prostration. In many locales this would be considered cruelty to animals.

In winter, the water outdoors for a dog can freeze and the dog can, too. Anticruelty laws require owners to provide adequate shelter for outdoor dogs against cold, heat and rain. Doing this properly will involve expense and planning.

Food left out for a dog to feed on freely can attract unwanted nighttime visitors such as skunks, possums and raccoons. The dog owner may never see these animals, but they expose the dog to rabies and other hazards. One night my neighbors' dog woke us all up barking incessantly. We discovered that a raccoon was on the fence post, with no intention of leaving. They took the dog indoors and the raccoon stayed for about two more hours, leaving a pile of feces on the outside of my windowsill as a parting gift! Another time we all woke up in the morning to the scent of skunk on the neighbors' dog. My indoor dogs were not involved in either of these dangerous incidents.

4.9 INDOORS

I feel that if I want to own a dog, I should live with the dog, not force others to live with it! Companion dogs belong indoors with their owners: any other arrangement is second best.

A dog that lives inside is much easier to keep clean. It is also easier to train and handle, because it has so much more contact with people. The wild behavior so common when the outdoor dog comes in for a short visit becomes greatly toned down when the dog lives inside. Much of that wildness is the dog's instinctive greeting ritual. When people are around all the time, they don't have to be greeted as much! When people regularly go out and come back in, the frequency of this event will cause them to teach the dog how to behave. Dogs are social animals, and their benefits to people occur when they are with us. A dog cannot be a companion when left alone in the backyard; it can do little to protect owner or home in the backyard, and it can quickly become less a member of the family and more a nuisance and liability. This is not the dog's fault.

Keeping the dog in the house and in a confined area for exercise will eliminate most, if not all, neighbor complaints. It will develop the dog's maximum potential as a companion, giving you the most advantages of dog ownership.

4.10   IDENTIFICATION TAGS

Wearing identification tags at all times can save a dog's life. One tag should be the numbered rabies vaccination tag from the veterinarian. This tag allows the dog to be identified even by telephone. Another tag should bear the owner's name, address and telephone number. If a lost dog is found when the veterinarian's office is closed, this tag can save its life. A dog lover might be out for a walk, find the lost dog and use that address to walk it straight to the owner's home. The rescuer might use the phone number on the tag to call the owner. If the Good Samaritan cannot reach owner or veterinarian right away and has no place to keep the dog, how will he or she be able to return it? Having it processed through a local animal shelter—where it might get hurt, contract a contagious disease or slip through the cracks and be euthanized—is not a good alternative to identification tags.

Each of my dogs also wears a tattoo tag. These are registered tattoos that can be found in the groin areas. If Saint lost his collar, his tattoo would still be there. If he still had his collar on when lost, the tattoo tag would alert would-be thieves that stealing him could get them caught. Laboratories are not supposed to use tattooed dogs for research. And if for some reason the veterinarian is closed and I cannot be reached by phone, the toll-free number of the tattoo registry is staffed twenty-four hours a day. That's extra insurance for Saint, which he has never needed, since he has never been lost. Have your dog tattooed. If *all* dogs were tattooed, we could check those tagless dogs' tummies and find their owners.

Some people who show their dogs do not keep collars (and tags) on them out of fear of marring show coats. Others have had dogs hurt themselves by catching their collars on crates and fences. Some dogs are worse than others about this, but the type of collar makes a difference.

Find a collar your dog can wear safely. I had to make one for Star's tags, because good tag collars for large, coated breeds are hard to find. Saint wears a sled-dog collar. When all dog owners decide to tag their dogs, more types of collars will become available.

4.11 A SECURE AREA

Somehow, a dog must be confined securely at all times. This includes on-leash with the owner, tied out in a proper location (but note that this method, when overused, leaves the dog vulnerable to injuring someone who approaches, the owner liable to damages, and in time can ruin the dog's temperament), confined to the house, confined within a car with windows sufficiently rolled up (the back of a pick-up truck is not confinement unless the dog is tethered there), within a fence from which the dog cannot escape or in a secure dog run. A crate can provide confinement for a short time, but it is not an appropriate place for a dog to live. Note, too, that confinement to an automobile on a hot day can quickly kill a dog from the heat that builds up so rapidly inside a closed car.

If for some reason a dog cannot remain indoors all the time, the best alternative is a secure run. There are dogs that can chew through chain-link fencing, but for most dogs a run built of a substantial gauge of suitable fencing, with a top to keep the dog from climbing out and sufficient construction to keep the dog from digging out, is a good start. The run should have a long rather than square shape to encourage the dog to exercise. It should be placed so that barking will not disturb neighbors and should be cleaned at least once a day.

My dogs live in the house, and I have a fenced backyard, but a few years ago we decided that wasn't quite enough. We built a second, inexpensive fence of welded wire around the back door for the dogs to use to relieve themselves. Now they cannot be teased from over the property-line fence, and they cannot get to a meter reader or other person who has entered the backyard without our knowledge. This has given me much peace of mind. I would recommend it to any dog owner who lives where other people can enter the yard, because it so greatly decreases risks.

However you confine your dog, there will be expenses. Building a deluxe run and installing a properly made doghouse would be expensive at first, but could prevent damage to your house or yard or injury to another person. Keeping your dog in the house means not having to build a doghouse, but there is a risk of damage to your home. A dog crate can help prevent that—but it costs something, too! Any way you look at it, there will be some expense to confining your dog responsibly and some of that expense will be unpredictable. Properly confining the dog is the heart of a dog owner's responsibility. If it is possible to keep the dog in the house and provide the necessary training, dog ownership may not be cheaper, but the owner has the best possible chance of a good relationship with the dog, the neighbors and the law.

A crate will safely confine a dog for up to a few hours at a time to prevent damage to your home. It will also act as a safe, humane way of controlling a dog in an automobile.

5

Owning Multiple Dogs

SOME dog owners would never consider owning more than one dog at a time. For years I thought that would always be my choice. Other people feel that a dog needs another dog for a companion, and certainly dogs can find happiness in this way, if all the conditions are right. But many dogs are happier with only people for companionship. Dog owners with one dog can join forces to provide playtimes for their dogs with suitable canine friends, overcoming any potential disadvantage of having only one dog in a household.

Many people do, for various reasons, decide to own multiple dogs. This can be a happy life-style with good planning, or a nightmare when things go wrong.

5.1 AREA ZONING RESTRICTIONS

Before moving to any specific property and before acquiring any dog, research the zoning regulations concerning the number of dogs that can be kept on the property. Don't assume that what was true five years ago is still true now. It is common for people who have lived for years ''in the country'' to become slowly surrounded with other residents and to lose their previous rights to own any kind and number of animals they desired. Laws vary, but the general trend is not in favor of the resident who was there first. Instead, that resident can be required either to give up animals or to move out as others move in and zoning regulations change. New residents want to fully use and enjoy their properties free of noise, odor and other conditions that can accompany the presence of animals, especially animals with irresponsible owners.

Responsible dog owners can sometimes qualify for special licenses to keep more dogs than the zoning restriction allows, if neighbors do not object. Typically all neighbors within a certain radius of the property would receive written notice of your application and the time and manner in which to respond with objections or other comments. Neighbors tend to respond in the negative, unless they know you and respect the way you live with your dogs. If you are trying to buy a property, you will be dealing with neighbors who do not know you. Do not buy the property until the zoning problem has been worked out, since the risk is high that you will lose.

In a case of encroachment by new residents on an existing dog owner, action is not likely to be taken unless the new residents have a complaint. You can greatly improve your chances of living happily in your neighborhood with your dogs if you behave preventively so that neighbors have no cause to be unhappy about your dogs. If your dogs are securely confined, if you pick up and dispose of their waste in such a manner that it does not create an odor neighbors can smell from their properties, and if you make sure neighbors are not disturbed by noise from your dogs, neighbors are not likely to complain just because they know you have more than the allowable number of dogs. Occasionally there is a grudge that has nothing to do with the dogs, but most people are too busy with their own problems to spend time trying to make life more miserable than necessary for their neighbors.

For those who acquire more dogs than their property zoning allows, whether they knew of the zoning limit or not, the law can act swiftly and give them little time to find other homes for the extra dogs before confiscating them. That's why it's so important to do your best to avoid getting into this situation with your dogs in the first place.

Don't take the word of a realtor or any other secondhand information on this important matter. You probably won't have to give your name when you telephone the proper authorities and ask about the zoning for your area. However, to determine all the covenants that might be in effect for the particular property, you may have to identify yourself and the exact address of the property. This could alert people to watch later to see if you do move there with more than the allowed number of dogs.

Think ahead, too. Some zoning restrictions will not allow an extra dog even to visit, and boarding a dog for a family member could thus precipitate a crisis. If you plan to have dogs visit, leave room in your allowable population for them.

Many kennel owners struggle with zoning problems, and sometimes the best they can do is to dodge inspectors until they can move. One solution for breeders is to place some dogs on co-ownership, or having them live in private homes. This can mean happier lives for the dogs, too.

Zoning restrictions are one of many reasons why breeders sometimes have to find new homes for dogs they have kept for several years to breed. Every dog, no matter what plans people have for it, should receive in puppyhood and throughout life the socialization needed to enable it to adjust to a new home. When this is done, the retired breeding dog can go from kennel life to idyllic retirement as a companion. Everyone benefits, including the new owner, who receives a mature dog with behavior more easily managed than that of a puppy, and quite possibly a dog of greater beauty than the owner would have been able to afford if purchased as a puppy.

Limiting yourself to the number of dogs that zoning for your property allows does not guarantee that neighbors will not complain or authorities will not take action. Dog ownership is legally regulated in other respects besides the number owned. However, if you own an illegal number of dogs, one complaint can result in suffering and even death for those dogs determined to be over the limit.

5.2 NOISE

Before acquiring any dog, consider how much it is likely to bark and how your property is situated for neighbors to hear the barking. There are special considerations about the barking of multiple dogs.

First, just the fact of an extra voice in the pack can add enough volume to make the noise carry farther than it did previously, so one more dog can take your neighbors from contentment to complaints.

Second, some dogs bark more than others. Adding a dog of one particular breed might greatly increase the noise level, while adding a dog of a different breed might increase it only a little. Dogs also stimulate each other to bark. How close are you to your own tolerance limit? How close are your neighbors to theirs?

My smallest dog barks when she is excited, for a variety of reasons. She is often a trigger to start the other dogs barking, and I vow that I will never own more than one dog of this type at a time! When I am out with Angel and arrive home, I hear no barking from inside the house. But if Angel is home, no matter which other dog is with her, there is barking.

Saint is fairly easily stimulated to bark, especially when he feels that a possible threat to the house needs to be investigated. Such "threats" may be of interest only to him! He will often bark just because Angel does, which can drive me crazy. Since they are in the house, they are not driving the neighbors crazy, and I can quiet them when I want to badly enough. Their barking is valuable because it does repel potential criminals. However, don't count on a barking dog to alert neighbors to a possible crime. Such dogs are ignored by neighbors because they bark indiscriminantly, and neighbors try to ignore the noise.

Star is the quietest of all and is the type of barker I prefer. She will join the pack to bark at a perceived threat and will bark an alarm if she is the first to notice something out of the ordinary, but she does not bark from sheer excitement. She also does not bark to get me to feed her, as the other two will on occasion. Instead, she uses endearing behavior to get my attention. If she is home with Angel when I return home from an outing with Saint, I will see Star's face at the window spotting me as I drive or walk up the driveway, but I will hear only Angel barking. When Star spots my husband or a friend through the window approaching the house, she does not bark but dances.

If these dogs had to live outdoors, Angel would single-mouthedly drive the neighbors crazy. Her barking may have contributed to her residence in the animal shelter where I found her. Saint could probably be tolerated, especially with good training. Star would not likely annoy anyone. These three dogs are fairly representative of the range of barkers that exist in dogdom. And don't count on a "barkless breed" to solve the problem. Barking is not the only way for a dog to make noise. When I had four neighbor dogs regularly howling together under my bedroom window, it was enough to almost levitate me off the bed! Some hound breeds have a musical baying voice specifically intended for the hunter to follow the pack of hounds by sound. It doesn't sound like music to angry neighbors, and it has astonishing carrying power.

Can you see the squirrel perched on the fence in the upper left corner of this picture (circle)? Squirrels are only one of many reasons dogs bark. Five minutes of barking in the daytime on a quick trip outside is not so bad, but I would never want to subject neighbors to my dogs barking outside all day. Prolonged barking at night, between 10 p.m. and 8 a.m., is illegal in some locales and is always disturbing to neighbors.

The potential noise is one reason for property zoning restrictions. If your property is small, it is likely that neighbors will suffer from noise when too many outdoor dogs live there. Some dog owners don't realize how miserable this is for neighbors. Having been on the receiving end of it, I wish I could convey the crazy, murderous thoughts I experienced! Noise is one form of torture used in wartime and certainly not something to inflict on our neighbors.

5.3 FIGHTING

If you have one dog and decide to acquire another, the last thing on your mind might be that they would fight. Civilized humans are governed by reason and rarely would parents decide not to have more children because their first child would not accept a sibling. Dogs, however, do not understand the complicated language it would require to explain to them why we want them to get along with each other. Dog owners can take actions that will promote harmony, but you cannot guarantee ahead of time that any two dogs will always get along. Some owner actions may even increase the risk of disaster.

One action you can take is to select your dogs carefully for compatibility with each other. My dogs are examples of such selections. Saint was first, an only dog for over two years. During that time he attended obedience classes, walked hundreds of miles with me in the neighborhood and had play dates with other dogs. He loved female dogs and was inclined, even with males, to work out a pecking order by play rather than by fighting. He had been neutered for almost two years and was under good off-leash obedience control when we decided to get another dog.

Our criteria when selecting Angel included size, sex and age. Having the dogs get along with no fighting was of primary importance. We got a small female dog and expressly avoided a terrier breed, since many terriers enjoy a dogfight. With a terrier the normal rules of dog interaction do not always apply. Other breeds have this nature, too, and you should research this when selecting a dog.

When dogs have normal attitudes toward other dogs, large dogs are inhibited by nature against harming dogs that are much smaller. Male dogs are also inhibited against harming female dogs. It is easy to see how these inhibitions would work in nature—both help a pack to live together harmoniously and to protect the young. When a female

Dogs fight for many reasons. It is cruel to keep two dogs together that fight. These two dogs are playing after obedience class. Notice the German Shepherd Dog making himself "shorter" to encourage his Basenji friend to play. Such experiences are good for the dog and help determine whether or not it could safely live with another dog of any size.

Some terriers can be aggressive and even enjoy fighting with other dogs. This places special responsibilities on their owners to be especially cautious around other dogs.

expresses aggression against a male, the male is inclined to give in to her rather than fight with her, an advantage in protecting her pups.

The inhibition against attacking a smaller dog may be related to the strong inhibition dogs have against harming puppies. This is of obvious importance to wolves, and it makes life easier for dog owners, too. Angel's small size—combined with her sex and Saint's attitudes toward other dogs—allowed her to make friends with Saint immediately. There are many such successful "Mutt and Jeff" size combinations of dogs in homes.

I was much more nervous when selecting a third dog, but Star surprised me by being so easy. She was abjectly submissive to other dogs and convinced all of us within fifteen minutes of arriving at the house that she would do her utmost to avoid a fight. Only a small minority of dogs are this submissive, and it is difficult if not impossible to diagnose a dog's degree of submissiveness on a single meeting. The majority of dogs will submit to some dogs and try to dominate others, and you will probably not know how your dog will react until you see it in that relationship. Some dogs are totally submissive toward all humans—that is not uncommon. But dogs that are submissive toward all other dogs are much less common. Unfortunately, dogs that attempt to dominate all other dogs they encounter are quite common, and if such dogs are large they should live only with skillful and highly responsible owners.

You can increase the chances of your dogs getting along by obedience-training each dog before you acquire the next and by introducing them for the first time in an area that is not home turf for either dog and that gives them a large space to interact in by running and playing. Each dog needs its own food dish, and there must be plenty of toys to go around. Don't give the dogs their dinner or a highly desirable chew toy (such as rawhide) unless you are there supervising. When you throw toys to multiple dogs, call out the name of each dog as you throw a toy to it, and immediately throw a toy for each other dog—in different directions. Do not tolerate fighting or jockeying for position near yourself—send all the dogs away if any dangerous interaction begins, and make it clear that you will decide when to pet each dog. Then proceed to pet all the dogs equally. Let them find out from experience that each of them will get a turn at all good things, including attention from you and time alone with you. If you do not have enough of something to go around, there will be problems.

What if you come home with a new dog and find that it begins fighting with your dog? Or what if your puppy got along with your older dog until it reached several months of age, or two or three years of age, but now they have begun to fight? Basically, you have two choices. You can find another home for one of the dogs. This is difficult and can mean a poor chance of the best life for the dog that goes to another home. But it would probably be my choice, because it can be so dangerous to live with two dogs always ready to fight.

The other choice is to keep the dogs separated, and this is often a necessary life-style for breeders. With the exception of a few breeds, dogs were not designed to live in large groups. Their nature is to form groups that their environment can support, and to drive off others, who then form new groups. That's what a dog's idea of territory is based on, and in nature with wolves it does not lead to fighting to the death. But when dogs are confined together by humans, the loser of the dominance challenge cannot go off and start its own pack. They will often fight to the death. For this reason, it is cruel to keep two dogs together if they do not get along. It is also dangerous, since people have been horribly injured (and a few children killed) trying to break up dogfights, and wounds from fights can kill dogs at the time or cause infections later, resulting in expensive veterinary bills.

So, you can establish separate quarters for the dogs, which usually means that your dogs no longer live indoors with you. You might rotate them into the house every day or every few days as some breeders do, but your life will change in a big way. You will not enjoy having an outdoor dog in your home as much as a regular house dog that stays clean and remembers its manners. This life-style also means reevaluating your premises, investing in dog runs or other accommodations for the dogs, dealing with potential noise and escape problems and having to provide adequate dog houses and bedding. In short, most of your way of life concerning your dogs will change.

All of this has a lot to do with why I would probably find another home for one of the dogs, but there is a clincher. It is common for dogs that are kept separated because they do not get along to get together on occasion. The cause could be anything from an escape to a situation the owner thought was under control that suddenly erupts into a fight, perhaps when the owner's attention is momentarily distracted. Then you find yourself in the middle of a nightmare. This is not how I would choose to live with dogs and is why the potential for fighting is something to determine before adding a new dog.

5.4 EXPENSE

There are many more expenses to consider with multiple dog ownership than the initial cost of buying another dog. There are few "economies of numbers" in dog ownership. A larger bag of dog food might be cheaper per pound, but it still needs to be of good quality or you will spend much more with the veterinarian, who seldom gives quantity discounts! Vaccinations, heartworm checks and medications and almost all other regular necessities will be multipled, not shared.

One expense that can be a shocker is when one dog contracts something that is contagious to the others. Instead of one sick dog, they can all get sick. When I adopted Angel from the animal shelter, she brought in some sort of viral bronchitis that Saint and my cats caught. Fortunately, it did not require veterinary care because each animal got over it in twelve to twenty-four hours, but it easily could have. On two or three occasions Angel and Star have both gotten minor sniffles after one of them went to a dog show, and I have had veterinary expenses from those infections. I carefully consider the risks of bringing a dog virus home whenever I take one of my dogs to an event where other dogs will be. I also avoid allowing my dogs to walk on grass away from home, because if one dog gets hookworms or whipworms there is a risk that all my dogs will get them, and viruses are also transmitted through dog feces found in such places as dog-show exercise yards. I did not have to be so extremely careful when Saint was my only dog: he never got sick from obedience class or other activities, although he did get fleas.

You might have a certain economy when it comes to flea treatment of your premises: if you have to do it for one dog, it may be no more expensive to treat the premises for more than one, excluding the products you have to buy for the dogs themselves. However, more dogs may cause more infestation of your property, which can mean having to treat the premises more often, and dog owners who have to do this know how unpleasant and expensive it is.

Consider also whether or not you can realistically afford to add a new dog to the family, especially in relation to its effect on the care you give to the other dogs. Many dog owners begin to neglect even

Here are some of the things you'll need to buy for a dog: a supply of dog food, a collar, a leash, a crate, some toys, food and water dishes, a soft bed, a breed book, a book and a tape on dog training, a comb, a brush, flea spray, vitamins, shampoo, rug and upholstery cleaner for pet stains, a nylon chew bone, nail clippers, pickup tools and three popular dog magazines. And don't forget veterinary expenses—they add up!

Clean-up and other chores of dog care continue through wind, rain, snow, mud—whatever the weather, the work is still there. The more dogs you have, the more work.

vaccinations when they get more dogs than they can afford. They would be much happier with the number of dogs they can care for properly, rather than having to live with the guilt of not taking good care of their dogs—to say nothing of the trouble poor care can cause. Overdue vaccinations lead to tragedy when all the dogs get sick, or when one dog bites someone and the dogs that are not current on their rabies vaccinations have to be put to death.

For breeds that require professional-caliber grooming, owning several dogs can create horrifying expenses. Breeders often learn to groom their own. Before acquiring more than one or two dogs that require professional care, it's time to learn how to groom. You might find that you lack the ability to learn the skill. If you do not wish to learn grooming, consider a breed that does not require it. Sometimes dogs of different breeds get along better than dogs of the same breed anyway, because a difference in breed can be an inequality that makes it more obvious to the dogs which one is dominant without a fight.

Another expense, if the dogs are to live together, is neutering. If you have not yet neutered your only dog, or your two females, you may find that the addition of another dog will make neutering everybody an immediate necessity in order to keep the peace. A neutered male can tie with and injure a female in heat. A spayed female can cause an intact male to become overprotective of the yard and bite someone. Hormones take time to adjust, so it's best to neuter existing dogs at least two months before acquiring another.

5.5   TIME

There is no economy of time in owning multiple dogs. Each of them needs regular individual attention, grooming, training and more.

If the dogs have to start living outdoors, you will need to spend time outdoors maintaining their quarters. It only takes me five minutes a day to clean the dog run where my house dogs relieve themselves, but going outdoors to feed, water and give other care for the dogs would seem a lot more work to me than doing the same chores in the house, where I don't have to get dirty. One breeder I spoke with mentioned keeping a set of grubby, smelly clothes that she wears for cleaning dog runs every day, and that her husband avoids her in that odorous outfit. I tried to imagine having to do that every day, but I really could not. How about you?

Could you give four dogs the individual attention each dog needs? Part of that regular attention needs to be away from the other dogs, one-on-one with you.

5.6   INDIVIDUAL ATTENTION

Besides the time required to give dogs their needed individual attention, the logistics are tricky. Now that I have had my three dogs for quite some time this has become part of my life-style, but it did not happen automatically.

When you first acquire a new dog, you may find that you have to separate your dogs to train or to play with them. They each need individual attention anyway, so separating them is worthwhile. Besides a training class for the new dog when it is ready, each dog needs to go away from the house alone with you at least once a week. It could be a walk in the neighborhood on leash, or a trip in the car to the drive-in window at the bank.

If you decide to confine one dog while playing with or training another at home, it is best to then take the confined dog out for a turn. Otherwise, interacting with one dog in the presence of the other could easily lead to jealousy toward the dog that got your attention. Unless you equalize the attention, it will disrupt the dogs' relationships with each other.

Now that my pack is running smoothly and all the dogs are trained, I can work with one or all of them without separating them. If I play with Star, Saint will probably be content for me to throw his ball for him afterward. Angel might want some excited verbalization from me, or a tossed toy, or her tummy rubbed. Or I might work one or more dogs on obedience commands or a new word I want them to learn, and end by giving all the dogs some praise and petting. No matter how well trained the dogs, when they behave well they need praise. The dogs that behaved well while I worked with the other dog have earned praise, too.

I also prevent jealousy by letting one dog help me train another. Saint might do a stay while Star heels, or Angel might demonstrate a command to help Star understand it or to give her confidence to try it. This gives both dogs individual attention without the trouble of separating them.

Each dog, however, also needs to leave the pack and have me to itself. One way I can give my dogs individual attention is to schedule their therapy dog visits to health-care facilities so that they are spread among all three dogs. It is best for the dogs that they not work too often (and also best for the program and for the people we visit).

Inevitably, though, the occasion arises when one dog is getting more attention and another less. Whenever I leave the house on an errand I consider whether or not a dog could safely go along, which dog would best fit the situation and which dog needs attention the most. If such an outing doesn't occur when one of the dogs needs time with me, I take that dog out for a walk. I do this by a schedule, not by watching for bad behavior in the dogs. Giving the dog attention must be done before the dog becomes emotionally needy, or it might take its feelings out on another dog.

Dogs do not obey you as a pack. They only obey as individuals. If you wish to keep them together as a way of life, separate them regularly and work on responses to commands. Otherwise you will lose control, and that's not good for them or for you.

5.7 EFFECT ON THE HOUSEHOLD

By now you have a good idea of the life-style changes that can occur as you add to your population of dogs. Anyone living in your home will be affected by these changes. Every new dog you acquire, beginning with the first one, brings not only some predictable changes to the household life-style but also unpredictable changes. Everyone deserves to be considered and consulted. Many homeless dogs and many divorces have resulted from dog owners who acquired too many dogs for their house-mates.

5.8 TOO MANY DOGS ELDERLY AT THE SAME TIME

As you acquire new dogs, give careful thought to the difference in their ages. Although the two-year intervals between my dogs worked well, they were not all the same age at adoption. The result is that Saint is only a year and a half older than Angel. As I write this, he is eleven and a half and she is ten. No one can predict how long either of them will be able to go out with me on therapy dog visits, but chances are they will both have to retire before much longer. To stay active in a particular task with dogs, spacing them well can make all the difference.

Worse than having to abstain from a favorite activity for a few years until you have another dog that can comfortably do it is the

Saint is 12, Angel 10½, Star 7½ years old. All my dogs are getting old at nearly the same time. In the future I plan to have dogs farther apart in age.

There are so many dogs to choose from, desperately waiting for homes. If you adopt that new dog you're thinking about now, are you giving up the chance to make a better choice later, when you may be better prepared? In haste are you risking creating yet another homeless, desperate dog?

emotional stress of having the dogs die close together. One of my neighbors, an active older lady, lost her two small dogs and her husband all within about a month. The emotional devastation is impossible to imagine, and her family and doctor were extremely concerned. To make matters worse, she was too grief-stricken to consider adopting another dog. Her doctor insisted that she keep a relative's cat. It worked, and she has remained active for several more years.

Pets can be vital to your health, especially when one is lost. Spacing your dogs well will help you cope with the inevitable losses. If you acquire the dog you may be considering now, will you be putting enough age difference between your dogs?

5.9   COULD YOU MAKE A BETTER CHOICE LATER?

I am glad to say that I could not be more pleased with each of my dogs. In any small way that one of them might miss perfection, there has been an opportunity for me to learn. They are all good dogs, and I would not have traded the experience of them for anything. I owe much of that to my husband, who made me wait a couple of years between them.

Two years might not be long enough for many people, or for myself in the future. I want five to seven years of age between my dogs from now on, in order to have a good chance of continuing to have a dog to work with as the oldest one retires. I have also found, as many dog owners have, that younger dogs in the group tend to invigorate the older dogs. I think for me it is a good idea to do as one friend suggested and get a new dog before rather than after the older one dies.

I have often seen dog enthusiasts acquire new dogs so quickly that the owner does not learn enough between dogs to make wise choices. Dog trainers live to regret this because they then do not have time to develop the potential of each dog and because they choose dogs that, with a few more years of experience, they would not have chosen.

Breeders have an equally serious problem when they acquire dogs before they have accumulated sufficient knowledge to choose them wisely. Their problem may be even more serious, because it can affect all those who acquire their puppies, not to mention the entire breed. Like the rest of us, breeders love their dogs and think they have the best dogs in the world. It takes years of experience and study to learn to make good matches when breeding dogs. Sometimes new breeders get lucky and acquire good dogs immediately after first becoming interested in breeding. But more often the established breeders with the best dogs and pups sit back and wait for the new enthusiasts to prove themselves with staying power and responsible decisions before offering their best breeding animals to them. Novices who acquire dogs too quickly may already have too many dogs before they are offered the best ones.

Worse, the new breeder may have established a bloodline he is attached to based on dogs he loved when he first started breeding; he might find, however, that these dogs have problems they are passing on to their offspring. It will be difficult to admit these shortcomings and start over, and many breeders don't have what it takes to do it. Then the breeder still must decide how to live with his dogs as the older breeding dogs age and can no longer breed—or as he realizes they should not be bred—and he wants new dogs to breed. Breeders probably have the hardest job of all dog owners in deciding how many dogs to own and in managing the changing population. Those who do it well are to be commended.

Whatever your situation, don't be too eager to add new dogs. Make sure you are sufficiently knowledgeable and have sufficiently developed the dogs you already own. Above all, don't expect a new dog to solve a behavior problem in your current dogs. More likely, the new dog will learn the naughty behavior.

5.10   WHAT'S BEST FOR THE DOGS?

I once got a call from an agency seeking advice for a client concerning two young male dogs of a small breed. They had been adopted together from the same litter and were now at puberty. The family who owned the dogs had previously owned two male littermates of the same breed and had been happy with them. These two, however, were behaving so badly that the family wanted them both put to sleep unless a home could be found for them together. The problem behavior? Relieving themselves in the house and chewing *very* valuable furnishings.

The best plan for these dogs would have been to separate them. They should not have been adopted together in the first place. They

The family that owns Fudge and MacKenzie feels that two Portuguese water dogs are exactly the right number of dogs and the right breed for them. Both dogs are conformation champions and are still active with their owners in other learning activities.

had bonded more to each other than to the humans in the family, with the more dominant dog inciting much of the behavior. With more maturity they also might have begun fighting.

However, the family mistakenly felt that the dogs would suffer more by being separated than by being put to death! There is something obscene about putting a healthy dog to death when a good home is available for it, as was the case with these two young, tiny dogs of a popular breed. The dogs would probably have been happier in separate homes: certainly the more submissive dog would have enjoyed getting out from under the constant dominance of his brother. Either dog might have made a great pet for the family and the other a great pet for another family. If the family continued to want two dogs, they could have properly trained the dog they kept and, after a couple of years went by, looked around for a suitable dog to come and live with him.

To do the best for the dogs, the owner and the family must be happy. Make sure that each dog fits your needs and capabilities. Ideally, find a breeder who will share the responsibility with you so that should the dog not work out with your other dogs, the breeder will have other homes waiting and will help you place the dog in a good one. If you adopt a mixed-breed dog from the shelter, you can increase its chances by giving it excellent training and socialization that would make it desirable to other people.

The best chance for the dog, though, is to stay with you, and to be exactly the right dog for you. Even when my dogs are old and retired they can enjoy leisurely walks, cuddling with each other around the house, telling me when it's their dinnertime and being in the kitchen when that unexpected but hoped-for piece of food hits the floor from a messy cook. I have been known to be a little messy on purpose, just to make a dog's day! My dogs deserve to have a happy old age. They deserve their share of my time, not to be pushed aside while I take on so many younger dogs that I have no time for their nightly grooming and other individual attentions.

I know that you, like me, want to do what is best for your dogs. It's a challenge sometimes to know what that is. One thing we do know is that dogs do not live happily together in groups that are too large or that are not compatible. This is a huge responsibility for dog owners, but it falls on us because the dogs cannot choose where they will live.

6

Grooming

IMAGINE a little child whose hair is combed only once a year, or prior to each holiday (when guests are coming), or before visits to the doctor. Anyone knowing of the situation would feel that intervention of some kind was needed, because that child is suffering from neglect. Insects could get established in the hair and scalp, and the child would be treated as a social outcast.

The same things are true of dogs that do not receive regular grooming. Groomers report that many dogs are brought in once a year, or before the holidays when the relatives will be in town, or before each visit to the veterinarian. The dogs are in such bad shape that it is impossible to groom them without subjecting them to miserable experiences. Insects, sores and even maggots are found under the matted hair. And these dogs are the ones that live in backyards, deprived of the social contact they crave and need.

I feel sorry for people who adopt dogs that require a lot of grooming without knowing what they are getting into, and I hope in this book to help people avoid that trap. But I feel much sorrier for the dogs. Veterinarians and dog groomers encounter this problem so often that they give up trying to persuade clients to care for their dogs properly. They also know that clients will often change professionals (out of guilt or embarrassment), and their concern for the dog will then lose them a client. Perhaps we can solve that problem for some dogs and people here by airing dirty secrets about the suffering of ungroomed dogs.

6.1 EXPENSE

Before selecting a dog for yourself that will require professional-caliber grooming, check thoroughly the costs of this service in your area. You might wish to visit some grooming shops for your research. Some may have a list of policies they can give you. Most will charge more for dogs in matted condition, dogs with parasites (because they require treatment in order to be allowed in the shop with the other dogs) and for larger dogs. Charges will also vary according to the type of coat and how it is groomed, since some procedures take much longer than others.

Many breeds require professional-caliber grooming. Question breeders and groomers before selecting a breed as to *exactly* what grooming will be required. Some breeds require an unbelievable amount of grooming that they will never get with most owners. In such a case the dog will never look or feel good, certainly not a life you want for your dog. Make no assumptions about grooming, because it is often not at all what the average person thinks of a certain breed, or what it appears when you look at it. A major problem when adopting a mixed-breed puppy is that no one knows exactly what grooming it will need as an adult. This creates many young adult homeless dogs.

In surveying dog groomers about the breed you are considering, ask also how often the dog should ideally come in for grooming. In most cases the answer is at least every four to eight weeks, depending on the length of the hair and the care you give at home between visits. The survey of prices and frequencies will give you some idea of the cost you would be committing to if you want to keep a dog of that breed groomed. This is an expense that lasts the life of the dog, through good and bad financial times for its owner.

6.2 TIME

Whether or not your dog requires professional grooming, it will need some of your time for home grooming. This could range

Standard Poodles require a serious commitment to grooming from their owners and care providers.

Bridgett, a Kerry Blue Terrier, visits her groomer once a month. Between visits her owners brush her every three or four days at home.

Basil, Wire Fox Terrier, requires stripping of his coat in preparation for the show ring. For private life he might be clipped instead, since clipping is more comfortable for the dog than stripping when done all at once by the groomer. Stripping is a special technique owners of harsh-coated show dogs usually master so that they can maintain their dogs to meet show schedules.

from five minutes a day for brushing and combing and other sessions during the week for trimming toenails and cleaning teeth, to hours every week to manage the coats of some breeds. Don't plan on spending *no* time on any breed, because they all require some grooming, in spite of what the occasional owner or breeder of a short-haired breed might tell you.

There is no one answer concerning the time you will spend bathing your dog, either, since coats vary. Many kinds of dog coats require no bathing at all if the dog is kept in a clean place and the hair is combed or brushed daily. Dogs do not perspire through the skin as people do, so the substances that need cleaning out are dirt that gets on them and excess oil that the skin of some breeds produces. One indication of whether or not a dog with excess oil will require bathing is whether the breed develops "doggy odor." If it does, occasional bathing will probably be needed. And it will be needed for a dog that participates heavily in outdoor activities.

Some people enjoy regularly combing or brushing dogs, but far more do not enjoy it or don't find the time, which is why the majority of dogs suffer grooming neglect. Dogs kept very clean are easier to groom, whether they live indoors or outdoors in a run. Sometimes people plan to keep their dogs indoors and select the breed accordingly, but put them outside later and find the grooming gets beyond their ability to cope. It is much more pleasant to spend a few minutes each day grooming a house dog than it is to handle a dirty outdoor dog, and it takes less time.

It would be helpful to ask breeders how much time they think it takes to groom the breed, but that answer may not help you much because breeders are not likely to groom their dogs in the same way that a responsible owner of a few companion dogs does. I timed Angel's daily combing session shortly after I got her and found that I was spending sixteen minutes a day. Now it's down to three minutes a day. I gained skill, Angel learned to turn and stand and hold positions as needed without wasting time and her coat is easier to groom after regular daily combing and after buying a better comb. If you start grooming your dog every day and it seems to take too long, take heart. Stick with it and the time will drop to a fraction of the time needed for a novice dog and owner to get through a grooming session; in fact, it will become a pleasant time with your dog.

Here is a Bichon Frise before and after a day of grooming to prepare for a conformation show. The fluffy appearance associated with the breed is not a simple matter of wash-and-wear.

6.3 EXPERTISE

If your dog requires clippers or stripping tools, you will need a fairly high level of expertise to do the job. That's why owners have such dogs groomed professionally. However, if you want to groom your own dog and are willing to learn to do it properly, over the long term you can save money. You can make your dog's life better if you can groom it thoroughly at home. A day at the grooming shop—or a half-day for puppies and old dogs—is at best tiring for the dog, and at worst an ordeal. For owners with several dogs that require this level of grooming, having all the dogs groomed professionally may be completely out of the question financially. Many professional groomers started out this way.

Another advantage of grooming the dog yourself is that some procedures result in a better coat if done a little at a time rather than all at once on grooming day. For a show dog, perfection in a coat is a way of life, not a short-term, just-before-the-show effort.

Many owners who try to groom their own dogs give up and return to a groomer with renewed appreciation for the skill involved! Don't try to learn without help. There are videotapes and books that may be useful for reference, but you will need someone to show you how.

6.4 EQUIPMENT

One reason owners who try to clip their own dogs give up on the effort is that they try to do it with equipment no professional would use. Don't buy anything to groom your dog with before consulting at least one professional groomer. A great deal of the equipment available is junk. Some pet shops have the right tools, whereas others have the worst. Besides pet shops, dog-show vendors' booths and mail-order catalogs are possible sources for grooming equipment after you get an expert to tell you exactly what you need.

Good clippers will allow you to change blades. Your dog will require particular blades for its type of coat, so consult a groomer before buying your blades. If your dog requires clipping, you may also wish to invest in a grooming table that will put the dog on a stable surface at a height that allows you to work accurately. Many dog owners want this even for brushing dogs that require no clipping, because they find it more comfortable and easier to manage the dog on

Fudge is retired from the conformation ring, and her groomer Carol is helping the owner learn to groom her at home. It is a challenge!

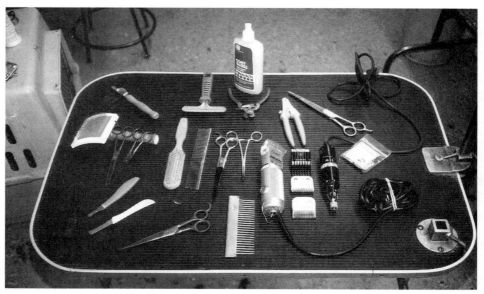

The right equipment is essential for effective grooming. Consult a professional handler or groomer before buying, so you can buy quality tools and won't waste money on the wrong equipment. This will make grooming more comfortable for your dog and give you a fair chance to develop your skills.

the table. You can improvise with a table and a rubber mat, damp towel, or rubber-backed rug to give the dog good footing. For my trained dogs that do not require extensive combing or any clipping, I drape a sheet over my lap and work there, but groomers tell me grooming in the lap does not work at all for many owners.

The selection of combs and brushes available for dogs can make you dizzy! Groomers, breeders and owners disagree on what is best, probably because there are so many different types of coats as well as owners who will groom them. I seldom use a brush anymore, preferring to use a Greyhound comb (a special comb for long or profuse coat) on my long-haired dogs, and my hands or a rubber curry on Saint. I also use the Greyhound comb on Saint to remove the loose hair that occasionally gets stuck in his coat instead of falling out. You will probably need to try more than one comb or brush before you find what you like best. If the extra tools are good ones, you'll find uses for them over the years in special circumstances or on other dogs.

6.5 CONSEQUENCES OF NEGLECT

It would be better not to have a dog than to neglect its grooming. It would also be better for the dog. A dog that is not properly groomed will not get the necessary petting it needs to remain a good companion dog. People will shy from petting the dirty and tangled dog, and the dog will shy from touch that can be painful. Skin can develop sores under the matted coat, and maggots can invade the skin, creating an emergency. Unless you groom your dog regularly, you will not know if it has fleas and ticks, which can endanger your own health.

Depending on the coat, an extremely ungroomed dog's behavior can deteriorate until it cannot be touched without biting, behavior that puts the dog's life at risk. Before bringing such a dog in for professional grooming, the humane process is to take it to a veterinarian to be shaved down, under anesthesia. Sometimes the behavior problem can be solved if the grooming is then faithfully maintained.

Dogs that do not visit the groomer often enough or are allowed to develop mats between visits will suffer at the grooming shop. This is not the fault of the groomer, but of the owner who does not give the dog proper care. Besides neglecting the coat in the first place, many owners demand that the groomer comb out a heavily matted coat rather than clip it. The dog suffers terribly during extensive combing of a

This Chow Chow in the animal shelter is severely matted. A dog in this condition is miserable and may resent being touched.

This Chow Chow has spent the day at his groomer's shop and is obviously enjoying himself!

matted coat. More than an hour of such work will be refused by many groomers as simply too much torture for the dog. Imagine yourself enduring an hour of having heavily tangled hair on your own head combed. By the time a dog's coat gets that tangled, it has been long neglected, and the skin underneath is so sensitive that combing makes it red and raw.

Groomers see dogs with parasites under the coat that are beyond belief. Ticks can bleed any dog to the point of death, and fleas can cause fatal anemia in small dogs and puppies. Many owners of infested dogs will argue with the groomer that the dog does not have parasites, but the fact is that these parasites, as well as maggots and tapeworms, are visible during grooming and often invisible to the untrained eye at any other time. Comb or brush your dog at home, and learn to recognize parasites so that you won't have to live with an infestation.

6.6 "PET" VS. SHOW GROOMING

When you selected your Poodle or Bichon Frise or other breed that regularly requires a date with the clippers, did you make your choice based on photographs of show dogs, visits to dog shows or perhaps a pleasant evening watching a dog show on television? If so, the reality of grooming may result in your dog having a very different appearance than that of the breed you thought you were selecting. In many breeds the type of clipping or stripping and the regular care required to maintain the coat for show is not feasible for most owners with their pets.

Stripping is a required process for many show terriers and takes much time and skill for many show terriers. The groomer will not want to put your dog through stripping on an all-at-once basis. If the dog is to be shown you will want to learn to strip it yourself in order to do it on the proper schedule. One reason that some show dogs live with professional handlers for extensive periods is so that the handlers can manage their coats between shows. Pet dogs with this type of coat are usually clipped instead of stripped. They will not then have the proper coat for show but will nonetheless be attractive, and periodic clipping by a groomer is much more comfortable for the dog than a rush job of stripping. A clipped coat will probably feel softer to the touch than a stripped coat, and owners may find that pleasant on their pets.

The length of coat required for some breeds to succeed in the

The white Poodle is in a Continental clip for show competition. Rubber bands hold the hair of her topknot and ears out of her way for daily activities. The black Poodle wears a retriever clip that is attractive for appearances in obedience trials. Either clip requires diligent attention, but the Continental clip is much more complicated to maintain and takes considerably more time.

show ring would be an unthinkable burden for many pet owners to maintain. Therefore, many breeds are commonly clipped much shorter for home life than their relatives are for show. That is not to say that you can't maintain a show coat if you want to badly enough. But to be fair to your dog, if you can't maintain the coat properly, you won't want to make your dog suffer by insisting on a cut that will become badly matted. Good intentions do not remove tangles.

These days I'm not much interested in fashion, but I remember high school days when dressing in style was so important to all of us. Every year we would look at the magazines and at first think the new fashions were ugly. The same was true of new styles in automobiles. But what you get used to looking at grows in its appeal, and every year we got used to the new styles and decided they were the best. Then the next year we went through the same process all over again.

The same visual effect occurs with our taste in dogs. You *can* grow to like the looks of the breeds that best fit your capabilities in training and grooming and the other responsibilities of owning a dog. And it will make for a happier life-style.

You can also learn to love the looks of your dog when it is groomed in a pet clip that is comfortable for the dog and easy for you to maintain. I find all dogs beautiful when they are healthy and well-behaved, especially if they are also friendly!

6.7 TOENAILS

Toenails tend to be an afterthought for dog owners, and dogs that see their groomers frequently can have their toenails trimmed then, too. However, dogs that do not visit groomers frequently for coat care need their toenails trimmed either by owners, veterinarians or groomers. I trim my dogs' toenails once a week to keep them from clicking or sliding on the floor without ever having to cut off so much at once that the nails would bleed. Show dogs need frequent toenail trimming for the same reason, since their nails need to be very short when exhibited.

Toenail trimming can be an ordeal for both owner and dog, and the only real solution is practice. A grooming table with a loop to hold the dog's head up while you trim may help—or a doorknob to fasten the leash. Having another person restrain the dog should not be your first choice since that is likely to make the dog struggle more. Another

Saki the Shih Tzu visits her groomer every two weeks. She seems to enjoy grooming, and this diligent attention allows her owners to maintain her in a beautiful long coat, which is a typical feature of the breed.

This Cocker Spaniel does not enjoy grooming. Her short, neat haircut is easier on her as well as on her groomer and her family.

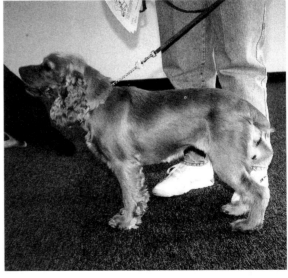

person can sometimes help by distracting the dog with treats. Approach the dog gradually, handle the paws gently and let the dog know that you will not quit. Don't let it turn into a fight, because then the dog will only learn to fight again next time.

If you feel in danger of your dog biting you when trying to trim its toenails, have the nails done professionally. Some dogs that run on concrete and do not have dewclaws will keep the nails worn down sufficiently without clipping, until, of course, they get old and less active. Trimming nails is a good skill to master if you can. Equipment makes a lot of difference. I used to dread and hate this job until I started using a scissors-type nail trimmer with two curved blades (instead of one) to grip the nail. You might prefer an electric nail grinder. Your veterinarian can show you where to cut when you trim your dog's nails.

6.8 COSMETIC SURGERY: TAILS, EARS

Since a dog uses its tail to express itself, I prefer to own dogs with intact tails. However, the removal of the tail is a brief process when done on very young puppies and poses minimal risk and trauma to the dog.

Ear cropping is another matter and is banned in some countries. To cause a dog's ears to stand when genetics made them pendant requires first a surgical procedure and then a period of aftercare that holds the ears erect. The aftercare is at best uncomfortable and at worst painful for the dog. The surgery should be done under a general anesthetic by a veterinarian, but some breeders do it themselves. So from the beginning there are dogs that suffer in order to have the conventional look for their breed. Increasingly, even show dogs can have uncropped ears and compete successfully, and in time all ear cropping may stop. Pet dogs do not need this procedure, and the weeks of aftercare can come at a critical time in a puppy's development, leaving it for life with a temperament that is not as good as it could have been. However, in many cases there is no noticeable problem for the dog at all.

When you adopt a puppy, the decision about tail-docking will have already been made, and you need not fear that it will have lasting detrimental effects on the dog, except in rare cases when the cut is done improperly. But ear cropping is usually done after most puppies are in their new homes, so it may be your decision, unless you have

Duke's ears have been cropped to make them stand erect as with most Great Danes.

Lady, a blue Great Dane, has natural ears.

Two Boxers—the dog on the left has surgically cropped ears, while its companion has natural ears.

the dog on a co-ownership and must share the decision with the other owner. Ears are cropped because of tradition and style, but just because something is traditional doesn't mean you have to do it, and style is a matter of what people get used to seeing. When an ear crop fails, the result is anything but stylish, and at some point is beyond repair.

This is a controversial issue, and it's best to make your decision before selecting a breed or a dog. If your dog is a mixed breed, if it has naturally erect ears, or if the breed standard calls for floppy ears, you can avoid the decision entirely. For breeds that by custom get ears cropped—or glued to produce a particular fold to the ear—the breeder may have strong feelings and so may you, especially when the time comes. Some dog owners who have had their dogs' ears cropped feel a responsibility to make the dog conform to its breed appearance and have not found the process difficult. Others say they would never do it again after having gone through the experience once. This is just one more decision when selecting the dog that's right for you.

6.9   THE DOG'S POINT OF VIEW

When I brought Angel home from the animal shelter in matted condition, I worked on her for what seemed like an hour to comb and cut out all the tangles. During the process, I promised her I would comb her every day so she would never have to go through this again. Now, eight-and-a-half years later, the only day we've missed was when she stayed overnight at the veterinary hospital.

I don't think Angel much cares for being combed out, but she lounges and relaxes and holds her positions because it is familiar and comfortable. In fact, she looks so content when I groom her that people enjoy watching. I think she knows that if she did not get this care she would get matted again.

I used to have to go get Angel to groom her, because she was reluctant to come. That's one reason I don't think it is her favorite activity. But after Star came to join our family, Angel had a change of attitude. Star's first owner was a groomer, and Star *loves* to be combed. She sighs, moans, snuggles and has a lovely time. So, being a pretty fair "dog psychologist," I deduced that Angel's me-too, me-first personality would respond differently to grooming if she thought she were getting something that Star wanted! I began grooming her first, with Star waiting to run eagerly into my arms as soon as it was her turn. No more need to go fetch Angel at grooming time!

Groomers tell me that dogs brought in for grooming regularly will often, as soon as they are dropped off by their owners, run right into the crates they usually spend most of the day in. They are eager to get in, seem to enjoy the day of grooming and are just as eager on the next visit. Nothing done at the grooming shop is painful for the dog if it is done at the proper intervals and the dog is free of mats.

In contrast, dogs that have horrible experiences because they come infrequently and in bad condition do not like grooming. They will experience pain with some procedures, because if the dog is too neglected pain can be unavoidable. They are also often the dogs that begin trying to bite groomers, and the biting behavior can carry over to other people when dogs grow defensive about being touched. Tragically, their temperaments can become so bad that they have to be euthanized.

Although grooming can be done humanely and can even be enjoyable for the dog, I think a case can be made for choosing a dog that does not need professional grooming at all. It is something an owner should consider before selecting a breed. When your dog spends time in a grooming shop, you cannot know exactly what happens or exactly how the dog feels about it. Experiences that can dramatically affect your dog's temperament are out of your control. The right groomer for that dog can actually help improve your dog's temperament, but it would be better if that groomer were you. Some dogs with coats that require clipping or stripping lack the constitution to endure it. In old age, standing on the table for the necessary length of time causes stress for many dogs.

If your only reason for desiring a breed of dog that requires professional grooming is that you don't think any other type of dog is as attractive, do take the time to further cultivate your tastes before selecting a dog. The choice you make will have profound effects on your life-style—and the dog's.

The best reason to choose a dog that requires clipping or stripping is when you need a dog that will have minimal shedding. Do thorough research if this is the situation, because just the fact that a breed *can* be clipped or stripped does not necessarily mean that the dog will not then shed. There is a range of dogs with this potential, so look also for the right size and temperament and other characteristics that will best fit you. Then, if regular sessions at the grooming shop mean the dog can live close to you in the house, it may be a trade-off that—if a dog could understand all the facts—it would gladly make.

MacKenzie has great affection for his groomer.

6.10 DAILY HANDLING BEST

If you ask the breeder or the groomer how often your dog needs to be brushed or combed, in most cases the answer will be once or twice a week. Done expertly this will suffice for many breeds, and a breeder may spend one entire day a week grooming kennel dogs. But the life-style of a breeder may not be the same as what you can provide for your dog at home. Combing or brushing all the tangles out of a dog that has not been groomed for a week might be beyond your ability. Soon you would quit trying, and you would have a matted dog.

The solution is to groom your dog every day. This has many other benefits as well, including keeping the dog tolerant of being handled and keeping you in close touch with your dog. It is the best way to know when your dog has parasites or if anything else is wrong with it, and it promotes a close relationship between owner and dog. It also makes the dog less sensitive about all handling, including combing. The fact that skin gets tougher when it is worked every day reduces the risk of the dog biting people out of sensitivity. If the dog has any sensitive spots on its body or former bad experiences from human touch, this regular procedure is the cure.

If you keep your dog combed out, you will reduce both the cost of any professional grooming the dog may need and the trauma it may inflict. You will be able to choose the length of coat that you prefer, not the length it has to be cut down to because of matting. Your dog's skin will stay healthier. Your dog will age more gracefully in health and behavior.

When Saint was about nine years old, I began including him in the daily grooming. Prior to that, I did not believe his short coat needed daily attention. I combed Angel and Star daily to prevent tangles in their long hair, but his hair was too short to tangle.

Because Saint was entering old age and still working as a therapy dog, I decided to start giving him a daily rubdown, requiring him to take and hold approximations of the various positions Angel and Star hold for combing. I thought the daily handling would be good for him and that he deserved as much attention from me as the other dogs, especially since he is not as prone to come and seek petting as they are.

I have been astonished by the benefits of including Saint in the daily grooming. It has made me realize how much we miss in developing our dogs to their potential.

First, Saint's already handsome coat developed a shine I would

If professional grooming means your dog can spend more time with you, that's a bargain most dogs would be happy to make.

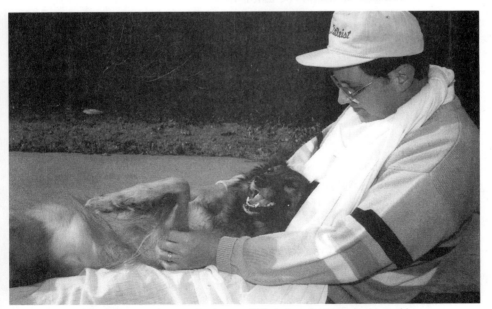

Her daily grooming session is one of Star's favorite things in the world.

119

not have believed possible. When a dog already looks great you may not expect daily grooming to improve the coat, but it is so good for the skin and hair that you are sure to see benefits.

Second, Saint had been my only dog with "doggy odor." He has oilier skin than my long-haired dogs, but both breeds are known to be free of odor. As I began the daily rubdowns, for the first few days a bad odor came from him during grooming. After perhaps a week this stopped, and his "doggy odor" I'd grown to accept as normal was noticeably gone. Distributing the oil daily from the skin onto the hair by rubdowns resulted in a glossier and sweeter-smelling dog.

One reason I began daily grooming for Saint at age nine was to reduce the risk that, with age, he would become defensive about being touched. It has worked! Within days of my starting the new grooming routine, my husband, who did not know I was doing it, began to remark on changes in Saint's behavior. Saint became more affectionate.

I had always tried to give Saint regular cuddling whether he asked for it or not, and had found this made him more responsive and more obedient all the time, not just during cuddling. The daily grooming dramatically increased this effect. If you have trouble getting your dog to listen to commands, daily grooming may help.

One reason it has this benefit is that when grooming the dog every day you command it to take each pose and to hold the pose until you give permission to move. You are practicing obedience command control as you groom. At the same time, daily grooming feels good to the dog—when the dog obeys a command, it gets the reward of feeling good through your touch. This is one of the things we humans can do for dogs that dogs cannot do for each other, and dogs desire human touch.

Saint's rubdowns took about fifteen minutes the first few days, as I taught him the positions I wanted. Now it takes about five minutes. He comes after Angel, and he's usually there before I finish with her.

Don't feel sorry for Star because she goes last. Dogs love pleasant daily rituals. As I spend time working on the other two dogs, she gets to anticipate her turn. When it comes, I start by giving her a warm hug that is as therapeutic for me as it is for her. Sometimes we end her grooming with "find the collar." I drop her collar down my shirt and she delicately locates it, pokes her nose between two shirt buttons and draws it gently out. Then there is praise and excitement—genuine, because I'm always impressed with that trick of hers. Being last for grooming definitely does not make Star least.

7

Care at Home and
with the Veterinarian

BEFORE a dog can be a well-trained companion that will give health to its owner, or be any kind of positive asset at all, that dog must receive proper care. Unfortunately, most dogs do not. Veterinary care is an expense, but many owners who could well afford it are frightened away by exaggerated notions of the cost.

Before deciding not to take your dog to a veterinarian, call area veterinary hospitals for prices of basic services. Not all charge the same fees, and if the fee is a problem, it is possible for the practice to work out payment schedules with you, especially if you become a regular client. It is best for your dog to have a regular doctor and to become familiar with the place. This familiarity will reduce stress on the dog and enable your veterinarian to provide you with better service and your dog with better care.

7.1 VACCINATIONS

Schedule a visit with the vet for vaccinations when you acquire a new dog. Call first to determine what vaccinations your dog will

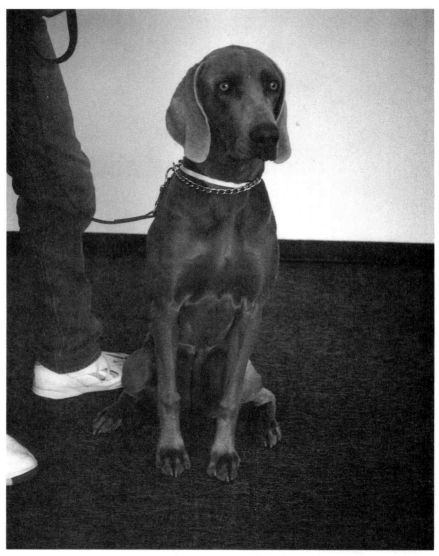

The companion dogs of today, like this lovely Weimaraner, enjoy the prospects of excellent health largely because of the advances that have been made in modern veterinary research. The responsible dog owner makes certain that the benefit of those advances are available to every dog in the house.

need. Have at hand any records you got with the dog. Even if the dog has already been vaccinated, chances are it will need one or more of the vaccines boosted by a second dose. If you have a regular veterinarian for other pets and are acquiring a dog that has already been vaccinated by another veterinarian, take the records to your veterinarian and get the dog's vaccinations—especially the rabies—on record there.

Why are vaccinations so important? There are several contagious diseases that kill many dogs for lack of vaccinations. Rabies can also kill people. Owners who do not vaccinate their dogs expose other people and their pets to the risk of *death*.

Some people save money by buying the serum and supplies and vaccinating their dogs themselves. But vaccine stored or administered improperly will not give needed protection. Only a veterinarian should vaccinate a dog against rabies, because the consequences of not having an official record of the rabies vaccination can be tragic. The assumption in such a case is that the vaccination cannot be trusted. The dog may have to be destroyed to be tested for rabies if anyone is injured. The alternative is expensive treatment for anyone who has been in contagious contact with the dog. The treatment can have dangerous side effects. The cost of the treatment for one human would more than pay for a lifetime of veterinary care for most dogs, and often more than one person is exposed.

Dogs seldom carry rabies. It is much more often carried by other animals. The concern is that dogs have closer contact with humans than most of the animals that are more likely to carry rabies, such as skunks. Nocturnal wildlife enters many urban areas completely unbeknownst to residents. If a dog is outdoors at night it can be exposed. If an unvaccinated dog bites a human—or causes broken skin in a way that can't be determined—that dog may be ordered destroyed for testing.

If a dog is hanging around your house and you are feeding it, perhaps trying to decide what to do with it, make sure the dog gets a rabies vaccination and other basic care, including confinement. You can be held responsible for a dog you feed. This is one of many ways in which stray dogs create problems. Feeding stray animals can be a misguided effort at kindness, attracting an animal away from its home when it might otherwise have gone back where the owners may have solved their confinement problem.

Some veterinarians offer low-cost vaccinations, and in some communities there is help for those who feel they cannot afford vaccinations for their dogs. Many epidemics among dogs are caused by the huge number of dog owners who do not have their dogs vaccinated. Young puppies have unpredictable gaps in immunity even when properly vaccinated, as do adult dogs that are ill or receiving immunotherapy (including steroids for skin problems and other conditions). Owners who neglect their dogs' vaccinations may be killing their neighbors' dogs. Regular vaccinations are essential to responsible dog ownership.

7.2 INTERNAL PARASITES

Many puppies come with passengers in the form of internal parasites. You might see roundworms in their feces, but the really dangerous parasites are not visible to the eye. Puppies and small adult dogs are at high risk of death from these parasites. Ask your veterinarian about treatment. For puppies, it may be desirable just to treat the dog without even examining a specimen of its feces. However, if it is not a puppy receiving routine treatment for this risk, bring a specimen for microscopic examination soon after acquiring the dog. If no parasites are found at that time, have another specimen checked between two and four weeks later. This will give any parasites the dog had acquired when you got it a chance to shed eggs that a fecal check can detect.

Fecal checks are not expensive. If you see anything suspicious about a stool your dog has left, especially a very fresh one, call your veterinarian. Moving worms in a stool that has just been deposited are probably tapeworms, which dogs get from fleas or eating wildlife. Scoop up a specimen and take it in within a very short time so the veterinarian can see the live worm. Treatment for tapeworms is simple.

Report to your veterinarian any blood in the stool, any indication that the dog feels pain, and any diarrhea that lasts for more than one or two bowel movements. All of these can be signs of internal parasites, or of other problems that need treatment.

Lacking symptoms, follow your veterinarian's recommendations as to a schedule of fecal checks. If you take excellent care of your dog's exercise area and the dog does not have occasion to walk on *any* other grass or dirt, the risk of internal parasites may be minimal. However, dogs can get some parasites by eating bird droppings, and there may be other wildlife in your yard that you don't see. Keeping dogs free of parasites requires diligent care.

What does controlling internal parasites have to do with respon-

A rabies vaccination must be administered to your dog by a veterinarian in order to provide proper protection. Consult local authorities about the required schedule—it's probably once a year.

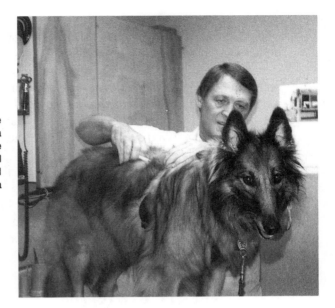

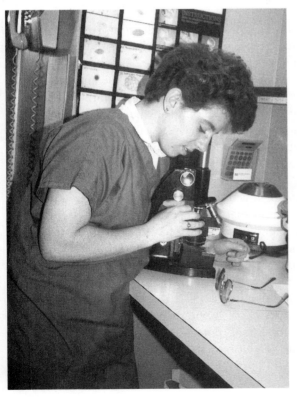

Some of the most dangerous internal parasites or worms your dog might be carrying can be seen only by a microscopic examination of a fecal specimen.

sible dog ownership? Again, this problem spreads to others. When a bowel movement from an infested dog stays on the soil, the eggs of the parasites infest that soil and thereby infest other dogs who use that area. You can also contaminate adjoining property. One example is when your dog has tapeworms and fleas and the fleas from your dog get on your neighbors' dogs—that's how tapeworms spread. Some internal parasites can even be transmitted to children who play on infested ground.

Heartworms are a special case of internal parasites often fatal to dogs. Treatment for a heartworm-infested dog is difficult. This disease is spread by mosquito bites, which is why it has spread so far and so rapidly. The best chances of treatment are in the early stages, before the dog shows symptoms. Use a preventive program your veterinarian recommends for your area.

7.3   EXTERNAL PARASITES

A major human health hazard that can result from irresponsible dog ownership is exposure to ticks. At a veterinarian's office, I had a demonstration of just how much ticks love dogs. Apparently a dog with ticks had been in the exam room before us. I saw the antennae of an insect around the edge of the wooden base of the examining table closest to where my dog Star was standing on the floor. It looked harmless, but there was nothing else to do while waiting for the veterinarian, so I got up to check. It was a tick, reaching and stretching for all it was worth, trying to get onto Star! The veterinarian disposed of it safely.

Ticks are attracted to dogs, whose metabolisms are different from those of humans. I have heard that it is because dogs run a higher normal body temperature than humans, and I have also heard that it is because dogs produce more carbon dioxide than humans with their breathing. Either way, ticks and fleas find dogs quickly. These nasty bloodsuckers would rather get onto a dog than onto you, but you will do in a pinch when they are hungry.

Various species of ticks carry Lyme disease, Rocky Mountain spotted fever and other conditions potentially dangerous and even deadly to dogs and people. If you find a tick on your dog, remove it and dispose of it properly. If your property becomes infested with ticks, it's an emergency.

126

Spray your dogs after outings to avoid bringing fleas or ticks home. Dips, flea-and-tick collars and shampoos are other alternatives. Consult your veterinarian about any product you use on the dog. Improper use of pesticides can be lethal.

When applying pesticides to your lawn, don't forget to wear rubber boots and gloves. Shower and change your clothes afterward. Better and less toxic products are continually being developed to control fleas and ticks. Your veterinarian and current dog magazines can help you stay informed.

127

Do not remove a tick with your fingers. Use tweezers or rubber gloves. If the tick discharges anything and that discharge makes its way into your bloodstream, you can be at great risk. People have died this way. There are various methods for disposing of ticks, but I usually submerge the tick in a glass jar filled with rubbing alcohol to be sure that it will be killed and will have no chance of crawling out. A tick flushed down a toilet can crawl out. Squashing the tick to kill it could expose you to the disease it carries—the blood can even squirt out and land in unpredictable places.

Anytime you treat your property for fleas, use a pesticide that also kills ticks. If you live in an area where fleas are a problem and you control fleas on your property, the ticks can be controlled at the same time in this manner.

Ticks and fleas thrive in shady areas and in high vegetation. I made the mistake of keeping a brush pile in a corner of my yard, which became a refuge for wildlife, and found it became a home for mice. Mice carry disease, and ticks that bite them can transmit disease to you or to your dog. After Star got sick following a tick bite, we eliminated the brush pile and the mice went away. That was the only tick we found on any of the dogs (it was well hidden in the webbing between two front toes), but she nearly died.

Improper use of pesticides can make dogs and people ill. Many people do not do a thorough job the first time, and, when it does not work, they repeat the treatment over and over. People have killed their dogs this way and made themselves ill. Your veterinarian can help you form a plan to treat your pets and property. You will need to use the correct products, follow directions, and repeat the treatments as indicated. With most products it's wise to wear waterproof shoes and rubber gloves when applying the treatment.

Fleas spread even more easily than ticks from one property to another, since ticks have to crawl but fleas can jump. I have heard some sad stories of fleas inflicted by negligent neighbors, and I have been the victim of that problem myself. People breed fleas on their dogs without realizing it, especially if the dogs have coats that conceal fleas.

A hard freeze kills fleas but can leave viable eggs to hatch out the following season. Opinions on what constitutes a hard freeze vary, but what a weather forecaster told me years ago has proven accurate in my experience: if the temperature stays below thirty degrees for forty-eight hours, the fleas outdoors are probably dead. If you still have fleas indoors, treat your dog and your house, and that is likely to eliminate them. Then treat the yard early the following spring. It is better to kill the fleas outdoors early in the fall so that there are none left to leave eggs for the following spring. In the hottest part of the summer fleas may stop hatching, giving dog owners a false sense of security. When autumn rains start and humidity increases, flea populations can explode as eggs hatch. The faster you respond to the first flea sighting, the easier the problem will be to solve.

There are substances other than pesticides that may help in the battle against fleas. Check with your veterinarian, groomer, garden center or extension service for up-to-date information for conditions in your area. Research is continuous, and new data is constantly coming to light. If people are not willing to use pesticides, lacking information on alternatives can then lead to doing nothing. In most locales fleas do not carry disease, but they are capable of it. Fleas only multiply when they have food—usually your dog's blood—so you don't want to be a flea breeder!

I have encountered people who put their dogs outside so as not to have fleas in the house, but it is easier to keep fleas off a house dog than to keep them off an outdoor dog. The right products and practices will give excellent results in keeping fleas from being able to reproduce in your house. Just sending the problem outside—and over into neighbors' yards—is not the answer.

7.4   DIET

Some veterinary expenses are caused by a poor diet. A dog does not need variety in its diet. When variety is created by an owner who buys this week's current cheapest-priced dog food, it can be disastrous. Changes in diet can give a dog diarrhea and chronic illness of the digestive tract.

First, find a good dog food that will give your dog the proper nutrition and then set about the task of getting the dog to eat it. When a dog is ill and missing meals could place it in possible danger, get veterinary advice on what special foods will tempt the dog to eat without doing it harm.

Most often, a dog's reluctance to eat dog food is the result of owners who give their dogs too many other snacks. Many foods will harm dogs and should never be given. Avoid giving your dog food

Don't worry, "Crummy Dummy Dog Food" is not a real brand. But inferior dog foods *do* exist, and can cause the problems listed on this label. Cheap dog food is *not* a bargain.

with sugar in it. Ice cream is not good for dogs. Satisfy your dog's craving for ice with ice cubes or crushed ice instead. Never feed them chocolate or onions—they are toxic to dogs. Avoid any food your veterinarian says your particular dog cannot handle, and avoid any food that has previously caused the dog to have diarrhea.

Talk to your veterinarian about the calories your dog needs. If you give the dog a scoop of ice cream when it begs for it, and it supplies the calories necessary to sustain that dog for a whole day, it is no wonder that the dog refuses its regular food. If you wish to cook for your dog, do it according to a balanced plan. Otherwise, make sure that the greatest part of your dog's diet is a high-quality dog food. Dogs derive most of their enjoyment of food from the smell. A tiny taste of a treat is better than a large amount.

Dog owners need to be aware that the dog-food industry is highly profitable and is *not* subject to the standards of human foods. Some dog-food manufacturers should go to jail for what they do to dogs with their cheap products. The easiest person to con is the person who expects to get something for nothing. The dog owner who feeds bargain dog food will pay extra at the veterinarian's office. Better to have a healthy dog and affordable veterinary expenses.

7.5 DAILY PICKUP

If you are a responsible dog owner, you will see your dog's food once more when you pick up the waste and dispose of it. If you wish to keep a healthy dog and disease-free property and be a responsible dog owner, the minimum frequency for picking up is once a week. The optimum frequency is once a day, which makes it a quick and easy chore and gives maximum disease and odor control.

There are many ways to dispose of dog feces. Some recommend that you bury it. Various doggy septic systems you can install in your backyard will dispose of the waste. There are also systems that will flush it into the sewer line.

I prefer to pick up with thin plastic produce bags purchased on a roll from the supermarket (ask the store manager or produce manager— these are very economical when bought on a bulk roll). I put my hand into the bag, wear it like a glove to pick up (I put both hands in if necessary to get a larger amount of waste), and turn it inside out to enclose the waste. I then tie the top into a knot. I try to pick up around noon, since it is easiest to see the ground then, with plenty of light but no sun in my eyes. It takes about five minutes to pick up in the run my dogs use to relieve themselves.

If the notion of discarding plastic for this purpose disturbs you, there are many alternatives. Paper towels will not stop the waste from reaching your hands if it is particularly messy that day. A scooper of any kind will require disinfecting—you might keep a bucket of solution to stand the scooper in until the next use. You could also save plastic bags from other purposes and recycle them for pickup before discarding. You could even have your friends and neighbors save them for you. With practice, you can probably manage with one or two bags a day, unless you have quite a few dogs. You will need more bags if you do not have a yard, since on property other than your own you need to pick up each time the dog relieves itself.

Squeamishness about picking up after your dog is the mark of an irresponsible dog owner. With practice you get used to this and give it no thought. What mother makes a big fuss about changing her baby's diaper, saying it is just too messy and she can't stand it so the baby will have to stay dirty? In a way dog waste is less ''dirty'' than human waste, because it has less potential to transmit disease to humans. Of course you should dispose of feces properly and wash your hands afterward, but it need not be a particularly messy job. It's pretty much just fresh dirt!

If you pick up daily, your property stays cleaner and you reduce the risk that worms and viruses will be spread from one dog to another. I had to learn this the hard way, when my tracking dog, Saint, picked up hookworms in the tracking fields and transmitted them via our property to Angel, who did not walk on the tracking fields. A good program of picking up regularly put a complete stop to this transmission, and from then on whenever Saint's fecal test was positive, Angel's remained negative. As veterinary medicine progressed, a medication became available that Saint could take to prevent him from getting hookworms. If your dogs are exposed regularly to internal parasites, you may wish to consider one of the available preventive medicines. Even if you have only one dog, picking up prevents the spread of disease and odor, and you will be glad of this practice if your dog ever does pick up worms away from home. If you do not pick up, by the time you find out the dog has worms, your property can already be infested. If you have been picking up faithfully, the dog can be

Here's the plastic-bag method of picking up after your dog, with a laundry detergent cap representing the droppings. Place the bag over your hand. In a stiff wind, use the other hand to steady the bag. If the volume of stool is large, put both hands into the bag.

With your hand gloved by the plastic bag, pick up the droppings.

Turn the bag inside out and secure the top—here the top is tied into a knot, but you might prefer to use a wire tie if your bag is of stiffer plastic.

treated much more easily without becoming reinfested from your own property.

Sunlight discourages the reproduction of parasites—worms as well as fleas and ticks—and also helps disinfect viruses. If you have a choice, have your dog relieve itself in an area that gets some sunshine every day.

Some people don't realize that they can train their dogs to relieve themselves in a particular area. In case you have this problem, perhaps I can make your life easier. Decide where you want your dog to relieve itself. If your whole backyard is okay, so be it. But if you live in housing where you must walk the dog to relieve itself, you can make this less of an ordeal. If you have a yard but want to be able to take your dog out for walks and not have to pick up constantly, this is for you, too.

Ever wonder why police dogs and guide dogs don't walk down the street relieving themselves at will? This basic training is available to every dog owner. Each time you take your dog out to relieve itself, go to the area you have set aside for that purpose and give the dog a cue word of your choice. Some say "Hurry up." If the dog wants to romp before responding or if you have a walk planned, go on with that. If the weather is unpleasant and the dog wants to go right in (not if you want to go in, but if the dog does!), then let it. Give the dog the reward it wants for having done what you want. Be very consistent about doing this every time. If the dog starts to relieve itself on the walk or while playing in the rest of the yard, interrupt it and return it to your designated area and prompt it to finish there.

Always praise your dog for eliminating in the designated area. If the dog goes for a walk or romps in the yard after relieving itself in the right place, give it another chance after the exercise before you bring it back into the house. Make it a faithful habit when you take your dog out that you take it to the designated area first and last on every outing. Let the dog discover it can count on this. If you continue this practice of praising the dog for using the right place and interrupting it when it starts to use the wrong place, you will soon find that you don't have to pick up on walks anymore. Always carry your pickup materials, though, for a dog could be ill or some unforeseen situation could arise. A wadded-up plastic bag or two is no burden to carry.

If you have your dog out for a prolonged outing and it must relieve itself, choose an appropriate spot, give the cue word and clean up. Don't leave it to the dog to just finally have to give in to an overwhelming urge. If you give the command in this situation, it will not harm your dog's training.

In case you're wondering how to interrupt your dog from relieving itself in the wrong place, the answer is to make it move! If you are walking and the dog just cannot hold it anymore and squats right there, stop only long enough for the dog to finish and for you to pick up, and then move on. A dog is more likely to want to "defend" territory it has marked with its own waste. As you develop your dog's habit of relieving itself at home before and after each walk, you also make the dog less aggressive on walks.

7.6 MESSES IN THE HOUSE

Occasionally there is a story in the news about authorities going into a home in response to neighbor complaints and finding it filled with dog waste. Most dog owners have far less of a problem than this, but responsible dog ownership does demand good control of the situation, and some dog owners are sincerely at a loss.

First of all, please understand that successful housetraining is not done violently. Most problems arise from not keeping to a schedule or not letting the dog out often enough and giving it enough time to respond. If you stick to a good schedule, take your dog out faithfully and encourage it to relieve itself before coming back in, this problem is likely to disappear. Be sure to clean the indoor area properly so that the dog is not led by its nose to use the same spot again. White vinegar is one way to discourage this. Do not leave your dog alone in any area where it is not yet reliable.

Also, do not expect a puppy to be reliable until it has the physical maturity to hold its waste, which occurs when it is between three and four months of age. You can see that quite a problem can be established if an owner acquires an eight-week-old puppy, does not properly de-odorize spots where the puppy messes in the house, does not limit the puppy to certain areas and does not take the puppy out regularly and encourage it to use the proper area. By the time the pup is old enough to have physical control, it will have established bad habits. Amazingly, dogs do seem able to relearn, however, so don't give up.

Families have a tendency to expect other members to take the dog out, while the dog dances around until it can wait no longer. In my house the first one up, the last one to bed and the closest one to the back door are first in line to let the dogs out at the proper times. That's only two adults—the more people in the house, the more confusion. It is a well-established fact that a human accepts more responsibility when he or she is the only one around. If you want a clean house, you'll have to be that someone!

When you catch the dog in the act, don't waste time punishing it. If you can hustle the dog outside and praise it for finishing there, you will have really taught the dog something.

If the dog makes a mess in the house, which will happen even with housebroken dogs when they are ill, the mess must be cleaned up immediately. There are many fine products for this, but paper towels or old bath towels, water, soap, disinfectant (if the dog is sick) and white vinegar will do. Pick up all the mess you can; scrub the area with water and soap; rinse with plain water; if carpet is involved, blot by stepping on paper towels, bath towels or old newspapers; then put enough white vinegar on the area to penetrate as far as the waste did. This will leave the smell of vinegar in the air for a while in the case of a deep carpet mess, but the end result will be no odor, and the dog will not want to mark on that spot again. You can substitute a bacterial enzyme odor eliminator: these products will work even on messes that were not deodorized promptly, while vinegar often will not.

Some breeds are more difficult to housebreak, so consider this in your choice of dogs. Your floor covering can also greatly ease the clean-up chore. No one enjoys jumping up and cleaning messes at the inconvenient times they seem to occur, but that is the task of a responsible dog owner—unless you want to become one of those bizarre news stories!

7.7 EMERGENCIES, ILLNESSES

Your relationship with your veterinarian becomes most important when a dog is ill or injured. The better the veterinarian knows you and your dog, the more smoothly the situation can be handled. Under the veterinarian's instructions, you may be able to perform care at home that otherwise would have to be done in the hospital. You can prevent many emergencies by the regular check-ups your dog gets at vaccination time and by good care at home. Dogs owned by responsible owners do not have to die of parasitic infestation or conditions that have been neglected for so long that it's too late to treat them.

Detergent, old newspapers, paper towels, white vinegar and an old bath towel are main-stays for cleaning up a dog mess in the house. Never use ammonia on dog urine, because its scent encourages the dog to mark the spot again. The scent of vinegar dis-courages the dog and neutralizes the odor. If urine has remained for a long time, you will need a product containing a bacterial enzyme odor eliminator.

When visits to the veterinarian are routine, you and your dog will both function better when you are there in a crisis situation.

Angel (looking through car window) is comfortable at her doctor's office. She knows he'll probably give her a treat—I bring along small bits of cheese for the purpose.

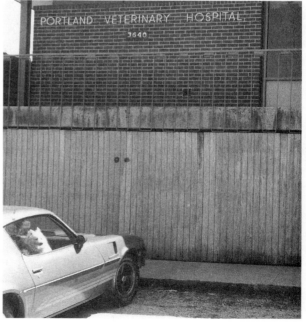

Vaccinating your dog will eliminate the risk of fatal diseases such as parvovirus. Keeping your dog properly confined will prevent it from being hit by a car or shot by a neighbor for chasing livestock. Picking up after your dog every day will alert you to any changes in its stools.

You can also protect your dog by not keeping two dogs together that fight. If an aggressive dog is getting into your fenced yard where your dog is, take action. Begin by contacting the dog's owner, and if that doesn't work, make an official complaint. Dogs have been killed in their own backyards, or horribly and expensively injured by fence-jumping strays. Talk to such dogs' owners first and let them see how upset you are, without turning it into a personal attack. Approached in this way, many people will act responsibly. They may not be aware of the problem until you tell them.

If your dog is in pain, don't delay consulting a veterinarian. If cost is a factor, the veterinarian will do everything possible to help. You may be surprised to find that the solution is simple and inexpensive. If you cannot afford expensive testing, tell the veterinarian—he or she is used to dealing with this. Do not attempt to diagnose the dog's problem yourself. You would be wise to invest in a current dog-owner's veterinary guide to help decide when the dog needs to see the veterinarian immediately. If you cannot afford such a guide, you can borrow one at the local library. Or call a veterinarian.

Most veterinarians practice sensible, economically priced medicine, and dogs benefit immeasurably from their services. Veterinarians are also responsive to human needs—more so than some doctors who treat humans! Form a relationship with a veterinarian, and let him or her help take proper care of your dog.

Animal shelters are filled with young adult dogs whose owners gave them up when they were no longer cute little puppies. It's not fair to acquire a puppy unless you really want the dog it will become.

A wide board secured across the threshold of the gate can help prevent this type of escape. People and dogs step over the board, eliminating the hollowed-out area under the gate that forms another exit for small dogs.

8

When Is It Time
to Give Up?

8.1 WHEN IT TURNS OUT TO BE MORE
COMMITMENT THAN YOU EXPECTED

This chapter will discuss the more common reasons many people
get rid of their dogs. The same circumstances occur to many other dog
owners who do not respond by getting rid of their dogs. Responsible
dog ownership is a commitment. The time to make that commitment
is before acquiring a dog and altering its life forever. Adopting a dog
must not be a spur-of-the-moment decision, based on the availability
of an attractive dog or puppy or some emotional low in the person's
life. The novelty of having a puppy will wear off, and life will change.
The initial commitment must go beyond the moment or the next few
months.

However, you may have a dog now that you cannot handle, or
you may face one of the following situations in the future. Considering
these problems and the options for dealing with them may help you
avoid giving up your dog. It may also help you choose a more suitable
dog the next time.

8.2 CONFINEMENT PROBLEMS

Many dogs can go out of the backyard at will. I suspect that most dogs could, given enough incentive. If you can't keep your dog in 100 percent of the time, when is it time to give up?

First, don't blame the dog. Many terrific dogs would be escaping from backyards if they were left outside, and I expect mine would be among them. I have never given them enough time alone in the yard to learn how to escape. A smart, sociable, active dog requires adequate confinement. Companion animals such as dogs belong in the house. Second best to the house is a secure outdoor or indoor kennel. Don't be surprised if plans to keep a dog loose and unattended in a backyard do not work. Whatever you do, don't get rid of one dog that gets out of the yard, and then get another dog, thinking that it was the first dog's fault. The next dog will probably get out, too.

Second, once the dog has formed the habit of getting out, a different fence may be an expensive failure. The money would be better spent in providing escape-proof accommodations for the dog, either in the house or in a secure run.

8.3 NOISE

What if you have a dog in your backyard—or in your apartment or in a secure dog run—that makes too much noise and the neighbors are unhappy? The topic is discussed earlier, but when is it time to give up? What are your choices?

Well, dogs bark, and I would not acquire a dog in the first place in a situation where the sound would disturb neighbors. The potential for noise is a problem that few dogs owners seem to consider until someone complains. A different dog is not the solution at this point, because your neighbors are already upset and will be even quicker to complain at the next dog's barking.

Many trainers claim success in training dogs not to bark, and you can buy books on the subject and work on the problem that way. In the meantime, let your neighbors know what you are doing and if there is any way they can help. For example, if the dog is barking at them when they are outdoors in their own yards, it would be a good idea to help them make friends with your dog. This would also reduce the risk of the dog biting them someday.

When a "successful" escape puts the dog in contact with a postal carrier, the encounter may not be this friendly.

When a dog is dangerous, everyone suffers, especially the dog.

Difficult as it might be, if you live in an apartment with a barking dog, my suggestion is to try to move to a free-standing house. The apartment dog is already accustomed to living indoors, and eliminating the walls, ceilings and floors shared with neighbors should solve the problem, especially if windows in the house are kept closed and heating and air-conditioning systems regulate the temperature. For an open-windows person, add to the housing requirement enough space between neighbors that a dog barking through a window will not disturb them.

An alternative suggestion would be to have the dog debarked. This is a controversial procedure, and if you decide to consider it, get recommendations from knowledgeable breeders in the area to find a veterinarian who has success with the surgery. It can cause complications, but otherwise dogs do not seem to mind it. In fact, they may be much happier, allowed to make their little coughing sounds without rebuke.

If the dog is outdoors and disturbing neighbors, the solution is to move the dog indoors. At least let the dog sleep in a garage or utility room between 10 P.M. and 8 A.M. when people are asleep. But better yet, retrain the dog as a house dog. Some owners say their dogs prefer to be outdoors, but this is only because the dogs have not been indoors enough to get used to it.

If you are a breeder or for some other reason must house some dogs outdoors, it may be time to move to a more rural area. Take care in the choice of a new home. Because residential housing may someday encroach on any rural property, consider that in the size of the property you buy as well as its location and other particulars. Make sure it is large enough and the kennel situated far enough away from property lines that noise will not disturb neighbors. Sometimes, however, geography can work against you and make noise carry an incredible distance. If possible, build a kennel that will prevent the sound of barking from carrying. You probably will not wish to listen to the noise a kennel full of dogs can make any more than neighbors will.

8.4 THE DANGEROUS DOG

What if your dog's bark is not worse than its bite? What if you have seen your dog do something dangerous or neighbors complain that the dog is dangerous? Do not ignore this problem, because it will probably get worse.

Consult your veterinarian and any dog trainers that are available to you. The fee for services charged by a dog trainer is not much of a guide to the value of those services, so get recommendations before trusting anyone with your dog's life and your safety. Contact the breeder before you get rid of the dog or have it put to sleep. It's better to include the breeder in your problem from the beginning, since a responsible breeder can be the person most qualified to determine the dog's temperament and to advise you. If the breeder that produced your dog is not sufficiently knowledgeable and responsible, seek the advice of others who know the breed.

Professionals are not always correct in their advice regarding euthanasia. In making a decision, here are some points to remember:

1. The dog's behavior is not the dog's fault. In rare cases there is a genetic or other physical defect. Most of the time the problem is improper handling or the wrong dog for that particular owner. The dog has no choice about any of these things, so it is completely inappropriate to blame the dog.
2. Act *immediately* to deal with the problem at the first sign of dangerous behavior. This might be as basic as your puppy's teeth marks on some member of the family. If early behaviors are changed—and that almost always means changing human behavior—you may never have to make any heart-wrenching decisions regarding your dog's behavior.
3. Get a good diagnosis of what is making your dog dangerous. This is essential to your dog's future and your future as a dog owner.
4. If your dog is dangerous, the only people you can responsibly pass it on to is the breeder, a police department, a military force or a trainer. Do not pass on a dog you think is dangerous to anyone except an expert handler.
5. If you must put a dangerous dog to sleep or send it back to the breeder or to some other responsible party, do not go out and get the same type of dog again. You may not be suited for dog ownership. Research other types of pets. If a dog is what you want, consider a much smaller dog or a dog with no protection attitude, and get expert advice to help make your choice. Make your new dog a house dog and get training. Tell anyone who helps you choose and train the new dog what happened before, so you can avoid the same problems.

Taco the rose-breasted cockatoo has as much personality as a dog. Birds are popular pets, are therapeutic to their owners and are easily managed by many people who would have difficulty with dogs.

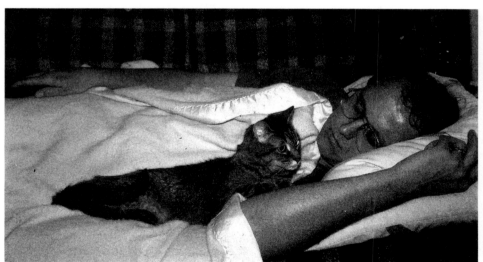

Cats now outnumber dogs in popularity as pets because their care is usually easier and less expensive. They provide companionship and other therapeutic benefits to their owners. Sissy is over eighteen years old—indoor cats can have long life spans.

8.5 "A HOME IN THE COUNTRY"

Prominent in the mythology of solving dog problems is the idea that some dogs need to live in a home in the country. Actually, the mythologists don't mean "in" such a home, but rather allowing the dog complete freedom to roam around outdoors. The fantasy is that if they just had enough room to run, the story would have a happy ending.

There is no such place. Lives for dogs left to run loose are just as short and ugly in the country as they are in the city. Hazards to humans from loose dogs are just as great in the country. Most responsible dog owners who live in the country already have more dogs than they can say grace over. Because animal control is sometimes not available in rural areas, residents often have the sad duty of shooting roaming dogs that menace people (especially children) and kill livestock.

8.6 MOVING

Some of the saddest dog ads are those that read, "Moving, can't take dog." There are circumstances when financial hardship dictates taking a home where you cannot have your dog. If the dogs of those who sincerely cannot keep them were the only ones animal welfare workers had to find homes for, they could probably do it. Unfortunately, too often the owner has little commitment to the dog in the first place and moving is an excuse to leave it behind.

I have a dog who had to be given up because the owner was moving, and she had been loved and cared for and treated like a little princess. When the owner could not keep her anymore, she notified the breeder immediately, and the dog flew into my waiting arms. She was cherished before and she is cherished now. If you will deal with a reputable breeder and do your best for your dog, such changes are possible. However, don't let this little story deceive you. If I had not wanted this dog, there were others waiting. Is your dog that desirable? Do you have a breeder standing by to help? My dog was never advertised in the newspaper. What kind of contacts do you have to help you find a home for your dog?

Is your dog a member of your family? If you would not move away and leave your child, are you sure you want to move away and leave your dog? If your situation is that grave, let others know and get help. For dogs owned by people who have to leave suddenly for military service, volunteers have stepped in to provide foster or perma-

Even dogs like this Briard that have been developed for herding could become a menace to livestock if allowed to run loose in a rural area. All dogs require responsible confinement, and the idea that a fence-jumping city dog can find happiness "in the country" is a fairy tale—without a happy ending.

L. D. Guy

If I move to a new home, Star moves with me!

nent homes. Compassionate family members and friends have provided for the dogs owned by people moving permanently into health-care facilities. If you might face such a situation, try to plan for this when you first acquire your dog or as soon as possible. Make your wishes known to those who would be involved in your care, and make arrangements for your dog. If authorities are forced to make the arrangements, the animal shelter may be the only choice, and for the dog it will be stressful and probably tragic.

8.7 PERSONAL OR FAMILY PROBLEMS

In cases of divorce and other crisis situations, dogs, like children, can be innocent victims. Sometimes these problems involve radical life-style changes.

If your dog is important to you, giving it up could harm your own health: in taking care of the dog you may also be doing what is best for yourself. Remember: dogs can adjust to many changes.

Sometimes breeders take dogs back for several months to help owners over rough patches. Breeders can help in ways that you would never expect, but first you must let the breeder know there is a problem. In fact, you should regularly report to the breeder about your dog.

It may be unreasonable to ask someone to keep your dog for an extended period of time and then give it back. Be sensitive to the other person's feelings if you become able to retrieve the dog. Some people will love having a dog for several months or a year and then being free of the responsibility again, while others will resent having to give the dog up and might suffer emotional stress. Get feelings out into the open and make the decision together. No one can know ahead of time how they will feel later.

When trying to find solutions to life-style changes in managing your dog, consider these possibilities:

1. If you will suddenly be away from home more often than before, consider installing a doggy door into a secure run, so that the dog does not have to wait for you to get home to relieve itself.
2. If staying someplace where the dog must be very quiet at night, consider training it to sleep in a crate in the room where you sleep. This can make a period of upheaval such as extended travel feasible.

Is your dog a member of the family? If you would not move away and leave your child, are you sure you want to move away and leave your dog?

Dogs often become innocent victims when marriages dissolve.

3. If the dog's feeding schedule must change, there are many options. My dogs have to change their schedule every time my husband goes out of town on business, because he normally feeds them at his bedtime and when he wakes up quite early in the morning. By the second day the dogs adjust to my schedule, which means more frequent feeding. Don't assume your dog is such a creature of habit that it can't do this. More frequent feeding helps us, and eases transitions. Another possibility is free-feeding, but only if you have one dog and it will not overeat. Or you can invest in a fancy feeder on a timer that opens only when it is time for the dog to eat. You can also change a dog's food, if you do it sensibly and gradually, to a form that is more feasible to feed in your changed circumstances. Consult a veterinarian about changing your dog's food or changing the time of feeding gradually enough that the dog won't suffer needlessly. Usually, if the new food is a good one, it will work well to change the food over a period of four days. The first day the feeding is 75 percent the old food and 25 percent the new food. The second day it's 50-50. The third day it's 25 percent the old food and 75 percent the new food, and the fourth day it's 100 percent the new food. But do call the veterinarian, because if your life and your dog's are under stress, the last thing you need is a dog sick from a change of diet the veterinarian could have told you would cause problems.

4. What about a dog-sitter? Neighbors can be irresponsible, but paid sitters can be excellent, as can relatives and dear friends (lucky you, if you have a neighbor who is either a relative or a dear friend or both!). Sitters can perform varied functions, depending on the need.

5. You can combine adjustments, a little bit of this and a little bit of that, to make a workable solution for getting through a difficult period. Dogs are far more adaptable than most people realize.

Sometimes people tend to throw things overboard at times of stress because they feel unable to cope. Experts say that is not wise. Don't make major life changes when you are under great stress if there is any other choice. Instead, try to find ways to continue your life, and your dog's life, as normally as possible. You may find healing for yourself in doing what's best for your dog.

8.8 THE SICK DOG

When should you give up on a sick dog? That's a very personal question. Don't let money be the only factor. First, try to decide what is best for the dog. Then if money is a problem, you may be able to work it out.

The increasing availability of expensive technology in veterinary medicine has presented some dog owners with difficult, even agonizing decisions. Those decisions can be made easier if you think about it from the dog's point of view.

Medical care is not a science. Different veterinarians will look at the same problem and suggest different solutions. It's not a good idea to jump from veterinarian to veterinarian because tests may then be duplicated, and decisions should be based on what has already been tried. Much as you may not want one veterinarian to know you are consulting another one, for your dog's sake you need to be honest with every veterinarian involved.

Form a relationship with a veterinarian whose judgment you trust. Establish communication so that the veterinarian will understand your priorities. For example, when my nineteen-year-old cat had cancer, I wanted her to be comfortable and to have the most peaceful death possible. It did not make sense to try heroic measures to cure the cancer, which was not likely to cause her much pain and was not likely to be curable, either. At her age it was not a question of living several more years, but of what failure in her body would be the one to end her life. This was an easier death than many other conditions would have caused. We gave her the best care we could for the four months she lived, and I held her when it was time for her life to be ended with a needle. If I were she, that's how I would have wanted it, which is not to say that I want to be euthanized under similar circumstances. The experience with the cat made me aware of the many motives relatives might have for wanting to have a human euthanized!

When Star was sick at age three we made a different choice and fought a long and expensive battle. She might have died or been disabled, but at her age she had a good chance of at least coping with disability, and it turned out that she didn't have to do even that.

Most illnesses are not so extreme. Often a visit to the veterinarian will solve the problem. If your veterinarian always seems to perform multiple, expensive tests that reveal very little, shop around for another

152

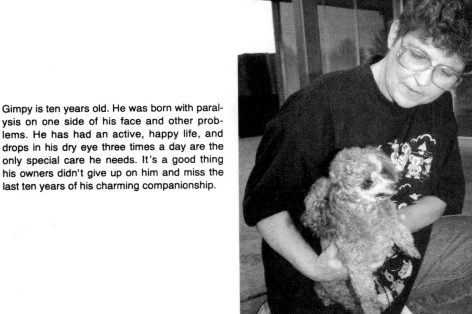

Gimpy is ten years old. He was born with paralysis on one side of his face and other problems. He has had an active, happy life, and drops in his dry eye three times a day are the only special care he needs. It's a good thing his owners didn't give up on him and miss the last ten years of his charming companionship.

Miniature poodle Ch. D. Two R. Two (D.R. to his friends) is fifteen years old and still enjoying life.

veterinarian. There are excellent diagnosticians in the veterinary profession who do not need an arsenal of tests for every simple case.

Even if you can afford expensive care for your dog, many tests are invasive, and the dog should not be put through any more pain, fear or stress than is necessary. I am convinced that Star did well because she was never hospitalized and treatment and testing were kept conservative.

Blood, urine and fecal tests are routine and need not be stressful for the dog. Learn to collect urine and fecal specimens at home. If other tests are recommended, make sure that you understand their purposes. Make sure, too, that you fully understand any medication your dog is taking, including possible side effects. Like human doctors, veterinarians can assume you know more than you do and forget to explain the purpose of a medication and how long a dog should be on it. Many owners keep their dogs on medication long after it should be discontinued. Others do not give the medication as directed, and then, of course, it cannot help the dog.

The difference between a good and a bad outcome when a dog is ill is often the nursing care you give. Be honest with the veterinarian as to what you can and cannot do. There are often alternate medications and treatments that can be used.

Did you know that dogs can wear diapers? Did you know there are carts made for either temporary or permanent use with dogs that suffer hind-end paralysis? Did you know that a dog can often get along fine with a missing leg? Don't jump to conclusions about what resources are available to cope with a dog's illness and the possible resulting disability. Discuss it fully with your veterinarian, and give yourself time to think and to discuss it with other members of the household before making any decisions. If you do your best for the dog, you need have no regrets.

8.10 THE ELDERLY DOG

Old dogs become more special, and still have much to give to owners who have loved them. It is hard to say good-bye, but the time has to come. If you plan for this natural time in your dog's life, it does not have to leave you so grief-stricken that you vow never to have another dog.

Life may have to change for the older dog, and you can help. The old dog should be petted, groomed and handled, perhaps even more than in earlier years. These pleasures can take the place of some of the more active fun the old dog is losing. At the same time, giving your dog this care keeps you aware of changes in its physical condition. Since the dog may have new aches and pains in aging joints, regular handling is important to keep it tolerant and comfortable about being touched. Otherwise old dogs sometimes begin to snap when petted by children and others they are unsure of. Frequent handling from you can make all the difference in your dog's adjustment to aging.

Some old dogs and their owners benefit from the addition of new young dogs to the household while the old dogs can still enjoy the company. Sometimes the younger dog offers protection for the older one, such as when an old dog loses its vision and a younger dog helps to guide it. But every case is unique, and some old dogs could not think of anything worse than to have to share you with a younger, stronger and more active dog.

Increasingly, as medicine becomes available to keep animals going longer, owners have to make the painful decision to have their old pets put to sleep. This was the case with my old cat, who in times past would have died of the initial infection that signaled her cancer. Instead, she was treated with antibiotics and wasted away for another four months before another infection brought her to a crisis and we decided not to put her through surgery for it.

Being old is not a disease, but disease often accompanies it. The question should not be how much money you are willing to spend or how much time you are willing to devote to care for your aging dog. The question is this: What would my dog want if it could understand what is happening? Dogs are all headed toward old age and death; and the minute a defect in the dog's health is first discovered is not the time to have it put to sleep if the dog is still comfortable. Some owners do this impulsively, thinking it will ease their own pain. But it does not. The dog should be allowed to live as long as it comfortably can. If you manage your dog's life this way, you will have less pain when your dog is gone. A hasty decision to shorten the period of dealing with the death ahead can greatly lengthen the period of grief afterward.

So, when is it time to give up on a dog? For some people, the time to give up is before getting a dog if the problems in this chapter are likely to be more than you can handle. But for many of us, doing what is right for our dogs makes us better and stronger people. Don't give up before you have the chance to experience that. Don't give up too soon.

Dog training is for all ages—of dogs and people.

Untrained small dogs are less potentially dangerous than untrained large dogs. It's a shame, though, to waste their full-sized brains by not training with them. Whenever I think Angel is too small to learn something, she likes to prove she can!

9

Training

T HE GREAT equalizer in responsible dog ownership is training. Trained dogs have a far better chance of succeeding in their homes and not being given up by their owners. When the dog has had its vaccinations and is healthy, it's time to start formal training. Puppy classes are highly effective and give puppies many social experiences they need for proper development.

A dog is never too old for training, provided it is tailored to each dog's needs. Unless you can manage to have a trainer permanently live with you (!), you will need to train *with* your dog. Improper handling at home will ruin the training of even the best dog.

The owner's responsibilities in training a dog vary according to the dog. It used to be that only people with difficult dogs and people who pursued special activities with their dogs were interested in training. That has changed. Excellent training is available for all dog owners, and is necessary for most. It may seem a big step to enroll in a training program with your dog, but if you find the right program, it will make a world of difference in your life and your dog's future.

9.1 THE SIZE OF THE DOG

Most people are seriously misinformed on the subject of the strength of dogs. Otherwise you wouldn't see so many small people with huge dogs. And there would be fewer cases of children dragged by large dogs when taking them out for walks.

Dogs are, pound for pound, approximately three times as strong as humans (some breeds are even stronger). A 45-pound dog is three times as strong as a 45-pound child. A small woman with a huge guard dog may be unable to restrain that dog.

If you have an especially large dog, training is the equalizer. A well-trained dog with a skilled handler changes the equation from one of strength to one of skill, respect and teamwork. Large dogs can be trained to assist people with disabilities who have little or no strength. However, not every dog has the character traits to learn to work with a human in this manner.

People who feel the need of protection are often drawn to the largest, toughest dogs they can find. When they can't control the dogs, everyone loses, especially the dogs. Consider your needs and capabilities when determining the size of the dog and the type of training you want.

There are tiny dogs bred for the purpose of serving as companions to humans in situations where larger dogs are unwelcome. For example, tiny dogs can fly in the passenger compartments of many airlines with their owners if the proper reservations are made, while larger dogs have to fly in cargo compartments. Tiny dogs are also permitted in many public places where larger dogs are not, often on an informal basis. On a hot day in the average community, it would be a hard-hearted shopkeeper indeed who would not allow an owner to bring a tiny dog in tucked under an arm, as long as the business is not one where dogs are prohibited by law, such as a restaurant or grocery store.

Tiny dogs are also more acceptable to landlords. It's not difficult to understand why. Tiny dogs can still transmit rabies, but other than that the small size of the dog reduces the risks of dog ownership in virtually every way. Tiny dogs do tinier amounts of damage when they chew the wrong things. Their bites do less harm to humans than do bites from larger dogs. Their housebreaking accidents are smaller. They may bark more than larger dogs, but their lungs, and consequently their barks, are smaller. If you were a landlord, what size dog would you prefer to take a chance on allowing a tenant to own?

Tiny dogs with training are delightful. You will need to modify somewhat the training techniques used for large dogs, and do lots of bending!

The larger the dog, the more training is needed if you are to enjoy your dog in public.

When it comes to training, the owner's responsibility is somewhat reduced with a tiny dog as opposed to a larger one. Training will still benefit the dog greatly, but owners will get into less trouble with untrained tiny dogs than with untrained larger dogs. Owners with small dogs have less responsibility—less liability—than owners with larger dogs. It's even easier to find a new home for a tiny dog than it is to find a new home for a larger dog when the need arises. The larger the dog, the more essential training is.

9.2 BREED PROPENSITIES

Breed propensities are important factors in the amount of training owners are responsible for. In other words, what type of behavior is typical of this breed? Is it a sporting (hunting) dog, with the propensity to spend all day running, a tendency that would be needed in the field? Is it a herding breed, designed to work all day, day after day, helping control livestock? These two types of dogs as well as many others tend to have high energy. When owners do not channel their dogs' energy properly, such breed characteristics can easily get dogs and owners into trouble. Some of these breeds were also bred to train readily, so an owner who desires to train and work with his or her dog may be well matched with such a dog.

On the other hand, an owner who is at work all day and, when at home, wants the dog to lie companionably around the living room in the evenings (after the dog has been inactive all day) while the owner watches television or does paperwork may have a problem. A working dog may be unable to remain so inactive and in its frustration may destroy property, repeatedly escape its confinement and otherwise behave in ways the owner will resent. A couch-potato owner may be much happier either with a couch-potato dog or with a dog that is small enough to get plenty of exercise just romping in the house.

If you wish to work your dog in public, such as taking it for walks or to dog events, consider how you would handle a dog that has the breed propensity of desiring to fight with other dogs. You would have to bring it under control through training before working it in public. Decide whether or not you wish to take on this responsibility.

If your dog has the instinct to guard property, you will have to train it and handle it carefully when you have guests—invited or otherwise—so that it does not attack the wrong person. Some such

160

Jerry the Pointer was found abandoned in a locked building at age five weeks. His owner works at home as a groomer, and he uses his Sporting-dog energy to play host to visitors.

dogs, while accompanying you for a drive, will also guard your vehicle, which is an extra responsibility when having your vehicle serviced, at drive-through businesses, and if you need to leave your dog in the car alone.

If the dog has the instinct to protect your person, you will have to properly educate the dog if you wish to have it around other people, otherwise it could mistake people's intentions when they innocently shake your hand or tap you on the shoulder. This training is a continuous process throughout the dog's life, since if it stays away from people too long it will lose the skill of properly interpreting human behavior.

There are other breed propensities to consider, but these are the major ones that involve training. For most owners, a dog that is moderate in its instincts is best. The most important thing to realize is that you can't just buy a dog with an instinct for a particular behavior and expect it to exercise that behavior properly on its own. All working dogs require proper training and handling. They generally require more expertise from their owners than is needed for dogs bred traditionally as companions. You'll be happiest if you choose a dog that fits your own ability and desire to train.

9.3   HUNTING AND OTHER SPECIAL JOBS

In order to understand your dog and handle it properly, find out if it was bred for a particular type of work. Research how a dog does that job and how a dog is trained for that job. Most such dogs will require some sort of outlet that is related to their instinct. You don't want your herding dog to decide to chase cars instead, or to slip up behind people and nip them in the rear. Retrieving tasks can satisfy these dogs. Your dog can learn to carry or fetch things for you and to chase and retrieve toys in regular play sessions with you.

If you have a job for a dog to do, it is most humane to choose the right dog for the job, rather than try to force a dog to work against its instincts. The right dog will be happier and more successful in the job.

Hunting is a job many dogs were bred for that has a bad reputation with some dog lovers. This is because of irresponsible hunters. Hunters have been known to mistreat their dogs while working them, to abandon them, and to treat wildlife with the same cruelty. However, it is not fair to judge hunting by the misbehavior of some hunters, or to condemn

162

Joe Bob, a young Pointer, is an active hunting dog. The pointing instinct is further shaped through training for control so that the dog can indicate birds in the field. After the game is shot, Joe Bob retrieves it. The retrieving done by hunting dogs provides for the most humane treatment of game animals and of the predators who can be harmed by eating shot in the game the hunter does not retrieve.

Responsible hunters love their dogs and take excellent care of them.

responsible hunters along with those who are not responsible (and in many instances are lawbreakers).

Vegetarians may understandably object to all hunting. But for humans who do eat meat, game animals properly managed and properly hunted do not suffer more than farm animals used for food, and in many cases have better lives and better deaths than farm animals.

Hunting dogs are used primarily to indicate game animals and to retrieve them after they have been shot. Provided the game animal will be eaten—which is the case with responsible hunters—it would be useless if chewed by a dog. Therefore, good hunting-dog prospects learn fairly easily to handle the game gently with their mouths. Saint demonstrated this for me as a young dog one night when he came in from a trip to the backyard with a tiny rodent in his mouth, uninjured.

The retrieving dogs (and most pointers also retrieve) help to spare game animals suffering. Without a dog, the hunter would at times not be able to locate or retrieve fallen game. Sometimes a wounded animal will run, in which case it is most humane to capture it and end its suffering. It is also important not to leave these, or killed game animals, out in the field for other animals to eat, because the shot in the crippled or killed animal could harm the predator that eats it. Properly trained dogs can find and get to game that human hunters cannot, and retrieve it to minimize suffering.

At times in human history, survival has depended on the skills of responsible hunters. That time may come again. Responsible hunters may be a minority, but responsible dog owners are also a minority. Instead of outlawing dog ownership because of those who handle it irresponsibly, we need to bring those people around to responsible behavior. The same is true of hunting. Most of the needed laws are already in place. What is needed now is not only better enforcement but also the force of educated public opinion.

If you wish to train your dog for hunting, you will need professional help. Choose a trainer with a humane reputation who will teach you how to keep up your dog's training.

The same is true of any job you wish to do with your dog. Police officers who work K–9 dogs have to train regularly with their dogs. Disabled people who receive already trained dogs to assist them have to take from two to four weeks of full-time instruction to learn how to handle their dogs, and most will have follow-up instruction and training after that.

One special job that is within the capabilities of a wide range of

Police K-9 dog Nick practices his off-lead heeling. There is no closer relationship than that between a K-9 handler and his canine partner.

Harriet has been trained to assist a deaf person by alerting to important sounds. A mixed breed, she was rescued and now she has a job, a motivation and enhanced outllook on life.

Guide-dog handlers work diligently to learn to handle their dogs and to stay in practice. Toni and her guide dog Ivy are a skilled team.   *Avigdar Adams*

dogs is that of therapy dog. Therapy dogs visit health-care facilities and give emotional aid to people. Your dog is still your dog, but on a regular schedule—perhaps once a week or once a month—it will go with you to minister to others. If this volunteer job interests you, the training described in the next chapter is a good start toward the skills needed for therapy-dog work. You will likely find a group in your community performing this service that will help you get started—or contact me through the publisher of this book, and I will help you!

9.4 COMPETITIVE EVENTS

Many dog owners find great satisfaction from participating in competitions with their dogs. Most events are connected with breed propensities and are designed to both test and express your dog's instincts. Some of these events are highly competitive, while others are run noncompetitively. The Canine Good Citizen Test described in the next chapter is an example of an event that is appropriate for all dogs and is not competitively ranked or scored. Such events put less pressure on those involved, and are less expensive than competitive events.

Breeders produce some of the best dogs in the world for competitive events, but most breeders' dogs are available as pets and companions since only a minority of dogs from any given litter will usually be suited for competition. These breeders tend to place their puppies conscientiously and to form the backbone of responsible dog breeding in any community.

While a few of the competitive events can quickly become too expensive for the average dog owner, many are quite affordable if you don't have to travel far from home to participate. Dog owners who start training their dogs with no intention of competing in formal events often find that they and their dogs enjoy such activities.

If you choose to train your dog for formal dog events, especially competitive ones, your success will probably be in direct relation to the quality of instruction you receive. One-on-one coaching is necessary for some of the highest levels of success. Use the finest instructor available. Your dog will be treated better by a knowledgeable instructor than if you retrain repeatedly in attempts to correct earlier training errors, and you will have greater success and more enjoyment in the activity.

9.5 TRAINING FOR PROBLEM SOLVING

If you have a serious problem with your dog or are considering getting rid of it, the first step is to get an accurate professional diagnosis of the problem. This might call for one session with a good trainer, your dog and your family. If you find the right trainer (one who can diagnose your problem accurately), a plan for correcting the problem should be possible from this meeting. Solving the problem usually means changing your handling of the dog and devoting a period of time to training under supervision. If the dog is dangerous, training should proceed with this or some other private trainer. If the dog is not dangerous, it may be preferable to train the dog in a class.

Sometimes you can enroll in a class with your problem dog and find success without a private trainer—if the dog is not a danger to other people or dogs in the class. This depends on the ability of the instructor to provide the personal attention you need while doing the same for other members of the class. Many "average" problems can be solved in a good basic dog-training class. Chances are good that the problem you think you have is actually a combination of things. The dog may not be precisely suited to your household, but don't despair—dogs are adaptable, and so are households! And you are also probably in the vast majority of dog owners who do not manage and handle their dogs properly, in which case a good class can seem to perform magic on your dog, when actually it is you who are learning the most!

If you have a specific problem driving you to seek training, find time to talk to the instructor before enrolling in the class. Express your problem and ask if the class is the appropriate place to work on it. There is probably more than one class available in your community, so interview more than one instructor before deciding. Unless your problem is an aggressive dog or you need coaching for a competitive activity, you will learn more in a class than in private instruction. In a class, you and your dog learn to work around other dogs and you learn from watching others learn and work.

9.6 TRAINING THE COMPANION DOG

You say your dog is a pet and doesn't need any training? That belief has landed many dogs in animal shelters, where most of them end up dying. To be successful in your home your dog has to be the right dog for the job—a dog you can reasonably expect to train and handle. Then the dog—and you—must train for the job.

What does a companion dog need to know? To some extent, that depends on your life-style and the dog's size and breed propensities. For example, it seldom matters if Angel jumps up on people and pats them on the knees, but few people want to be jumped on by Saint or Star, dogs large enough to tear their clothing or knock them down.

If jumping up on people would be a problem at your house, it will help you to know that the traditional methods of teaching a dog not to jump up don't usually work. In fact, most often training that is aimed at getting a dog *not* to do something is ineffective. What does work is to teach the dog the right behavior. The usual approach that really works with big dogs is to teach them to sit or to stand for petting. But you could teach the dog to lie down for petting if that was your need. The fun of companion-dog training is that it can be completely customized. In fact it will be, as you live with your dog.

You will probably also need to train a dog to relieve itself in a place most convenient for you. This is usually not addressed in dog-training classes, and may be learned in the first two weeks you own your dog. Before getting a dog, consult a veterinarian and a breeder and perhaps some written sources to decide where you will take your dog to relieve itself and on what schedule. If you have a fenced yard you may later be able to stand at the back door and watch the dog for the several times a day it needs to go out, but at first you will need to go out with the dog to supervise and encourage. Be sure to plan for this essential training time.

What about your dog's meal time? Do you plan to shut the dog in a crate for every meal, or will it eat in the kitchen with people around? Feeding time can be a special opportunity to practice training skills and keep relationships straight. For example, I have a separate dish for each dog, and they must take turns being served and must behave safely as they wait. Sometimes I have them practice ''Stays'' at various points of the process. They are eager to please—to hasten the serving of dinner—and practicing control when they are excited about being fed also helps with control at other times, too.

Your companion dog should wait at doors rather than rushing out everytime anyone opens a door. The same is true in the car. This is easily taught to a companion dog by a persistent owner who provides adequate practice for the dog and always enforces the rules. For example, even if the car is in the garage and the garage door is closed, if the dog jumps out before I give permission, I make the dog

Owners may not mind if their small dogs jump up and pat them on the knee, but it is a behavior best discouraged.

Duke could knock a person flat by jumping up! It may not be fair, but in many respects large dogs must be better trained than small dogs just to survive in modern society.

get back into the car and wait for permission. When a behavior is as important as this one, the key is always to stick to the same rules and to practice at every opportunity. Take that extra moment to put the dog back into the car, and insist that it wait for permission. Prevent the dog from carrying out the wrong behavior until it finally stops trying, and good behavior will become the habit.

What about lounging on the furniture? Is there someone in your home who absolutely cannot tolerate this? Then to make your dog acceptable in your home, you must *never* allow it on any furniture, or it will want to get up when no one is looking, and it will end up getting caught and in trouble. The only exceptions a dog could understand would be one of the following:

1. The dog is allowed on only *one* piece of furniture, and it is always okay for it to get up on that piece.
2. The dog is allowed to get on furniture only after a special spread has been placed on the furniture and you have given the dog permission.

While some dogs can understand such rules, if it will get your dog kicked out of the house to be caught on the furniture, the safest course is never, ever to let it on furniture and to provide it with its own cushioned bed. Some dogs need cushioning under their joints when resting, so this is a necessity, not a luxury.

To teach the dog to stay off furniture, you will need a bed for the dog from the beginning. When the dog tries to get up on furniture, take it straight to its own bed instead. The bed should be near you, so that obeying does not mean social isolation for the dog.

Your companion dog may need several other elements of training. Training does not mean yelling or hitting. It means teaching the dog how you want it to behave. That means you will first need to learn how to teach the dog the appropriate behavior for each situation.

9.7 COME WHEN CALLED

One command every dog needs to learn is to "Come" when you call. Owners create problems with this command that are much easier to prevent than to cure, so it deserves special attention here.

Problems result from calling the dog to punish it or to do something it doesn't like, such as giving it a pill or taking back dinner steak

Dutch has been trained to wait at the door instead of rushing through. He and his owners have practiced.

If any family member would object or if the dog shows any tendency toward overprotectiveness, the dog should not be allowed on your bed or other furniture. Be sure to provide a soft cushion or comfortable rug in the room where the people are, so that lying on the floor won't be a punishment.

Every dog needs to learn not to jump out of a car without permission. Star is particularly ladylike in the car—a real pleasure.

172

it has stolen. So rule number one for everyone in the household in handling the dog is that if you need the dog for something it will not like, *never* call the dog, *always* go get the dog.

The flip side of rule number one is that whenever you have something pleasant for the dog and the dog is not already with you, call "Saint, come!" Use the dog's name, pause slightly, then the word "Come!" Make your voice strong enough to carry, and use a positive tone that sounds the same every time you call. In an emergency, if you can calm yourself and get that same tone in your voice, your dog may come just out of habit.

The recall ("Come") is not the most reliable command for emergencies. When a dog is fighting, chasing, or otherwise fully engaged in an instinctive activity and pumped with adrenalin, you have a better chance of getting the dog to stop than of getting it to come. Skills discussed in the next chapter will help in that situation.

However, sometimes the recall will save your dog. Once Saint bumped into a rabbit when he and I were walking along the edge of some thick woods. His impulse to chase was irresistible, and as he lunged to take off the leash slipped from my hand. The woods were too thick for me to follow. I kept calling "Saint, come!" with all my heart. In one or two minutes he came running back to me. I was really proud of him and probably praised him longer than he had been gone!

For the best chance of getting your dog to you in such a crisis, practice the recall frequently in situations where the dog *will* come. Use treats, use pleasant daily rituals, use the leash, and practice, practice, practice. Do not practice failure by calling the dog when it may not come. Always be able to get the dog to you. Then the one time when it is all up to him, your Saint may come running back through the woods to you, too.

9.8 GUESTS

Guests are not a daily occurrence at my home, and three rowdy dogs are usually too much of a welcome, anyway! So my dogs greet guests on-leash and, after a calming-down period, can be off-leash to enjoy company, if appropriate. It is not reasonable to expect a service person who comes to the house on a professional call to deal with more than one leashed dog. I pick one dog before the visitor arrives (or when the doorbell rings) and put that dog on-leash to keep with me. I leave the other dogs in a comfortable area, depending on what parts of the house the worker will need to access. Sometimes the dogs rest in my car in the garage! The leashed dog gives me the personal security I want when alone in my home with a stranger and does not put the worker at unreasonable risk.

If it's a social visit, I look at how the person is dressed. Casual dress makes it reasonable for visitors to meet all the dogs if they want to, but if they are in dressy clothes I will discourage it, unless the visit is to be a long one. And if I feel a person would be unreliable with my dogs, I reserve the right to keep them away from that person. Accidents between a dog and guests in the home can cost the dog its life and the owner a huge lawsuit. The dog may be especially protective of the owner and of the home and behave differently than it would at other times. I work my dogs in public individually, but in a group at home they are a pack, rowdier than individual dogs.

If you are a guest in someone else's home, the responsible thing is never to take your dog unless invited to do so. This has caused friction in many extended families and friendships, but the least friction is caused by sensitive and responsible dog owners. People have many reasons for not wanting dogs to visit.

If you have many guests, and especially if you are unable to stop and leash your dog for greetings, you will need to teach the dog from puppyhood how to greet visitors without jumping on them. Do not wait until the habit of jumping up in greeting becomes established, or you may never succeed in changing it. The greeting is an instinctive behavior in dogs that comes out of the fact that they are highly social animals. Getting extremely excited when greeting—whether it is you returning home, someone stepping outside to the backyard dog, a guest arriving or another dog in the family returning home after an outing—is *normal* dog behavior you should not expect to change. What you may be able to change is the manner in which your dog greets. If you can conveniently leash the dog when company comes, you will find that the rowdy greeting lasts only five to fifteen minutes. After that, if the visit is social, you may be able to remove the leash.

9.9 GOING FOR WALKS

If you wish to take your dog out of the house for walks or other social outings, it will need much more training, and so will you! The trained behaviors of the Canine Good Citizen Test (see Chapter Ten) are ideal for this purpose.

Taking your dog for regular outings provides the chance for you and the dog to learn social skills together. I decided long ago that I wanted my dog to be welcome in the neighborhood, not disliked or feared when out on-leash with me. I began by encouraging Saint to be friendly in all situations and never punishing him when he was in the act of being friendly. As I got the other dogs, I handled them the same way, and this was instrumental to their becoming therapy dogs. If you want your dog to be protective of you, remember that it cannot recognize bad guys until it learns to recognize good guys! A dog must know how people are supposed to act before it can recognize dangerous behavior.

When you take your dog walking, you will need to pay special attention to its behavior around children: you will encounter them almost everywhere, and they are irresistibly drawn to dogs. Telling them not to pet the dog will not always work. If you have a problem in this area, get the help of a professional dog trainer before there is an accident. Dogs that injure children get into big trouble, and so do their owners.

If you want to take your dog walking, it must also be under control around other dogs. A training class is a good place to develop this skill. A good training class will include the basic skills needed to take your dog for enjoyable walks and will help you to assess whether or not this is a realistic goal for you and your dog.

9.10   SELECTING AN INSTRUCTOR

Before you can select the right instructor, you must determine your goals. However, goal setting may require some exposure to the activities that are available for you and your dog. If you acquire your dog as a puppy, a good puppy class will help you meet local trainers and other dog owners and help you find out what activities are conveniently located for you. If you miss the opportunity to work your puppy in a class, the chance to include this experience in your dog's development will never come again. Begin contacting area dog-training schools as soon as you decide to get a dog. There may be waiting lists, and your puppy needs to attend these classes at the proper age.

Puppy classes are usually safe places for dogs and owners, even if the instructors are not the best. But for any class other than a puppy class, you will need to choose an instructor qualified to help you train your particular dog in a humane manner. Success means having a dog you can control and enjoy.

Before trusting your adult dog to any instructor, get references. Your veterinarian may know if any clients have had particular success with or complaints about a trainer. The price of the program is no indication of its quality. Many low-cost training programs are taught by compassionate, dedicated and knowledgeable volunteers, while some expensive professional trainers ruin dogs.

Look for a trainer you feel understands your dog. The best indication of this is if you like the way he or she handles a personal dog that is in some important way similar to your dog. The right way to handle one dog can be the worst possible way to handle another dog, and some of the differences are breed-specific. Ask responsible breeders of your breed if there are particular trainers they recommend.

Use the phone book, the classified section of the newspaper, local pet shops, and every other lead to find a trainer. The best trainer for you may be the hardest to find. As more dog owners become aware of their training responsibilities, many more programs are becoming available. The quality of some is outstanding, while others are both rip-offs and cruel experiences for the dogs. If you run into one of the latter, don't give up on training, just give up—quickly—on that trainer.

Before taking a dog to any instructor, observe the instructor at work with other dogs. If it is a private session, ask the instructor to let you watch a session that is similar to how he or she expects to work with your dog. If you are not sure after watching once, attend more sessions as an observer. It is a small investment of your time, and a qualified instructor will not object as long as you do not bring your dog. There are no magical secrets to dog training that an instructor need guard—it is diligent, consistent, correct work that trains a dog.

Watch how the instructor handles people. Would this treatment help you learn? Would you be flustered or intimidated or impaired in learning? Would you feel comfortable asking questions?

How does the instructor handle dogs? Do you think the treatment is kind and fair? If not, look elsewhere. Old-style dog training tended to be rough, but those days are over. Make sure to choose an instructor who knows this.

When you determine your specific goals—such as problems in home life with your dog that you wish to solve, special training you

Obedience classes help dogs gain confidence. The first time Duke went over the A-frame, the instructor had to pull while the owner pushed. Here, just minutes later, he's taking it like a marine taking a hill!

Dogs are always learning—they can learn that dashing out the door leads to fun and games, or they can learn to wait safely for permission. Every interaction you have with your dog is a chance to teach the right things—once you learn how.

want your dog to have, or activities you wish to pursue—be sure to communicate these goals to your instructor and ask for guidance. A basic puppy course or Canine Good Citizen course is appropriate for any dog and owner, but beyond that you will need to find specialized training that fits your goals. Otherwise you will feel poorly motivated in class when working on skills that are not of importance to you, and you will be wasting time that would be better spent on your goals.

If you enjoy training your dog, don't give up too easily on finding the right activity for both of you. New activities are being added all the time, as there are infinite ways in which humans and dogs can form teams and accomplish goals. In the process, relationships become richer and deeper. And everything you learn with one dog prepares you for doing a better job with the next dog you own.

9.11   WHETHER YOU KNOW IT OR NOT!

Your dog is learning and you are learning to handle your dog every moment you spend together. If you do not get proper instruction, both of you will learn bad habits that can be difficult or impossible to change. Good dog handlers have dog after dog that is successful— whether as a companion or in some other job. It's not just that these people select good dogs, although that is usually part of the secret of success, but that they learn to handle each dog properly, getting the help they need for that dog. Each dog is an individual, and each dog needs the right experiences and the right handling in order to learn the right things. Otherwise the dog will still learn, but what it learns will be out of your control. The animal shelters are full of smart dogs who know things their former owners wished they didn't. The dogs are not to blame, any more than children who misbehave through lack of supervision and instruction are to blame. But, like children, dogs pay an even higher price than the adults who should have supervised and taught them.

Training is part of responsible dog ownership. There are two sure indicators that you are doing it right: One, the dog will be getting better and better behaved, and two, you and your dog will both be enjoying your interactions in training. It is not a chore to train a dog. It is an exciting and satisfying relationship.

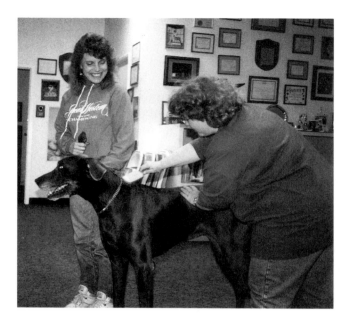

The Canine Good Citizen Test
begins with the Evaluator examining your dog as a veterinarian
or groomer might.

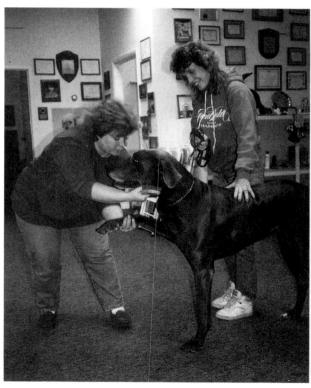

180

10

The Canine
Good Citizen Test

10.1 HOW THE TEST IS USED

The American Kennel Club instituted the Canine Good Citizen Test September 1, 1989. A major purpose of the test is to combat irresponsible dog ownership. To turn an irresponsible dog owner into a responsible one takes education. This test affords the American Kennel Club and all interested, qualified dog-training organizations the opportunity to reach out to dog owners and work with them, one on one, to educate. It also provides recognition in the form of a certificate for each dog that passes the test. The dog does not have to be an AKC-registered dog, and mixed-breed dogs are included.

Much about this test deserves praise from those who wish to see an improvement in how people behave with their dogs in public. Before the CGC Test was available, those who sought a standardized test of dog obedience were limited to competitive events designed for earning titles in obedience. Such events have brought about many positive changes in dog ownership, both in individual homes and in the nation, but not all dog owners wish to pursue such activities. The Canine Good

Citizen Test is not scored competitively like obedience trials. Some dog owners enjoy competition, but many do not.

Another advantage to the CGC Test is that it does not require as much expense and planning to test dogs and handlers as it does to put on a trial for them to compete in. You might compare this test to getting married by a justice of the peace or a presiding town judge, as opposed to an obedience trial, which is more like a formal wedding! Even an obedience match involves much planning and the help of many people. Some people like formal events, but those who don't enjoy them or can't afford them should still be able to get married—and they should still be able to test with their dogs, too.

But like that simple justice-of-the-peace wedding, you will need to prepare for the Canine Good Citizen Test. First, you train with your dog and develop a relationship that allows the two of you to work together. Do not attempt the test until you have prepared and have a reasonable chance of passing, since failure could make you feel dissatisfied with yourself and with your dog. This is not a test of the dog's basic "quality," but of socialization and training that dog and owner have worked out together.

You will also need to make an appointment with an Evaluator, who gives the test. Some Evaluators want to know you and your dog before administering the test, rather than rendering a decision based on an acquaintance of just a few minutes. If, for example, the Evaluator wants to meet with you and your dog at an obedience class the Evaluator teaches and have you attend some sessions with your dog before taking the test, you will obtain useful practice at the same time.

Unless a dog has a hopeless temperament (the percentage of dogs with that problem is small), it can be trained to take this test successfully. Some dogs will need a lot of training and others much less, but it is not a temperament test. It is a test of training and control. *Somebody* could probably train the dog. If that someone is not the owner, it's not the dog's fault.

Like other educational tools, the Canine Good Citizen Test can be expected to change in the future. However, as it stands today it is a tool to help determine whether or not an owner and his or her dog belong in public. This chapter will describe the ten basic elements of the test, what each element reveals about owner and dog, and some suggestions for training to help you master each of the skills.

10.2 APPEARANCE AND GROOMING

The test begins as you present your dog to the Evaluator for inspection. You show the Evaluator your dog's current rabies certificate (and any other vaccination certificates and licenses required where you live). The Evaluator checks to see that your dog is in good condition and is clean and groomed. The Evaluator lightly combs or brushes your dog and examines it, to make sure it will comfortably accept handling by someone such as a veterinarian.

Evaluators will behave as the individuals they are in administering this part as well as the rest of the test. Don't take your dog to an Evaluator for the test unless you are confident that it will be safe for the Evaluator to examine your dog and that the dog will not threaten the person or otherwise behave aggressively. If this seems to you to be a possibility with what you know of your dog, tell an instructor that you have this problem and enroll in a training program.

If your dog is timid when handled by strangers, it needs more positive experiences with them. Whenever it is safe and courteous to do so, introduce your dog to people you can trust to treat it gently. Some pet shops encourage you to bring your dog along for shopping there. You can find many other opportunities for your dog to meet people if you make this a priority. For example, guests to your home may be interested in meeting the dog, or you may stop in at the veterinarian's office during quiet hours and let office staff scratch behind the dog's ears and give it a treat, or you may take the dog along on some errands. Be sure not to impose your dog on people who do not want to be around it. If you have trouble finding people to help you socialize your dog, an obedience class should supply this need.

If at this point or any other time during the test the Evaluator feels that your dog is not safe for other people to handle, you will be excused and not allowed to continue. The same will happen if you handle your dog roughly.

10.3 ACCEPTING A STRANGER

On the next part of the test, the Evaluator will approach you, greet you and shake your hand in a pleasant manner. Your dog must more or less ignore the Evaluator, not going up to him or her, not showing resentment and not breaking position. You are allowed to

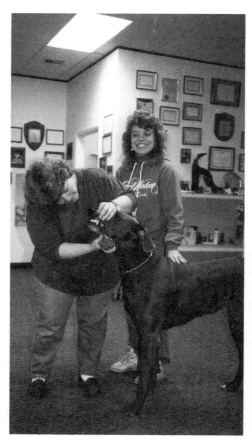

The second part of the test requires the dog to remain calmly at your side while the Evaluator approaches and shakes your hand.

speak to your dog just as you would when meeting people in public with your dog. You can tell your dog "Stay," and you can keep reminding it throughout the exercise.

A dog that has this skill can be prevented from jumping up on people in friendliness when out in public, or trying to "guard" the owner when meeting people. I remember a large dog that, at obedience events with its owner, consistently growled at people when the owner reached out to shake hands. This behavior was unsettling to me when the owner shook my hand, and he was concerned about it. The dog also had other problems and was retired early in its obedience career. In the hands of a less skilled owner, that dog could have been dangerous.

A dog that growls at all comers when in the company of its owner is demonstrating two things, neither desirable. First, the dog lacks confidence. A confident dog does not feel the need to threaten people, as long as they do not behave aggressively toward the owner. Second, the dog is demonstrating that it has not had sufficient social experience to learn to distinguish normal human behavior from behavior that represents a possible threat. If your dog has this problem, work with a trainer until it is clear that the dog is safe to be around, before you take it out in public.

If your dog has the opposite reaction and is so exuberant in greeting that it tries to jump up on the Evaluator, an obedience class will help you gain control. Then you can command your friendly dog to "Sit" and "Stay" while the Evaluator approaches. This is not as serious a problem as aggressiveness, but remember that a boisterous dog can knock someone down. If the person happens to be an older person with frail bones and poor recuperative powers, such an injury can mean the loss of the ability to walk and an early death. Since the owner can be liable for any action of the dog that results in injury to another person or damage to property, this is an important skill for owner and dog to learn together.

10.4 WALKING ON LOOSE LEAD
OR OUT FOR A WALK

Now the Evaluator will begin to put you and your dog through your paces, requiring you to walk together in a controlled manner with the dog on-leash, but no pressure should be used on the leash from either you or the dog. You will be required to execute a left turn, right turn, about turn, and two halts.

This is not a formal heeling exercise, and you are allowed to talk to your dog as much as you want. The advantages of training your dog to heel are many. It will enable you to move your dog from one place to another in daily life with a minimum of stress. It also teaches the dog to work with you as its leader. This is a healthy dog-owner relationship, and every time you practice heeling you have the opportunity to enforce this concept in your dog's mind, without unkind treatment.

Heeling also shifts your dog into working gear and its attention onto you. It is appropriate that it occurs early in the test, because it prepares the dog for the later exercises. It also allows the Evaluator to determine if the dog is under control and if dog and owner have a reasonable working relationship.

In daily life you can use heeling to settle your dog in a situation that overly excites it. For example, if you are out for a leisurely walk, letting the dog sniff around and think its own thoughts, and you spot a cat or a squirrel you think your dog would want to chase, you can alert your dog to walk at your heel and keep its attention on you. You can also alter your course to require the dog to pay closer attention in order to keep pace with you. That will take its attention off the squirrel and onto following you: the leader. Heeling is an antidote for anything that might distract your dog. It is a powerful exercise, valuable to all dog owners.

The test requires the dog to work on the handler's left side, but not to remain in perfect heel position as required in competitive obedience trials. The level of heeling needed for obedience trials requires a considerable amount of training and practice, but dog and handler can learn the work required for the Canine Good Citizen Test in a fairly short time. Dogs have various attitudes toward this exercise, and you may need an instructor if your dog is one of the extremes. Some dogs try to pull out ahead and are persistent about it. Your dog might require a slip collar for training, which is allowed during the CGC Test. If your dog needs any training collar, you should learn how to use it from an instructor, not on your own. Improper use of a training collar can harm your dog.

The other major problem dogs have in heeling is lagging. A lagging dog often has the opposite temperament from a dog that pulls out ahead, and needs more encouragement from its handler. Instead of

186

Dog and handler must walk together with the lead loose on the third section of the test—notice that the clip attaching Lady's lead to her collar is hanging vertically because there is no tension on the lead.

rebuking the dog, use a pleasant, excited voice to encourage it to come closer to you. Move briskly, and make extra right turns and about turns in practice (with the dog that pulls ahead, make lots of left turns and stop frequently). When the dog is lagging and you encourage it up to you, speed up—people have a tendency to slow down at this point, which conditions dogs to lag even more. Do not focus your full attention on heeling for more than a few minutes at a time—five minutes is enough. Your test will be shorter than that. Overly long periods of heeling, where the dog must pay close attention to keep the lead loose, will make it more difficult for the dog to maintain the necessary level of attention, and handler attention wanders, too. The net result is that the heeling work deteriorates.

Many trainers successfully use food treats for heeling training. You are not allowed to use food on the CGC Test and, of course, for daily life you need to train your dog to the point that it will obey you without food. If you used food in basic training, you must wean the dog off it until it is, at most, an occasional treat after your dog understands an exercise. High-precision obedience competition training is another matter, and food may be used much more to take the dog's mind off the fact that there is no real reason for responding with such precision. CGC training does not require such precision but is meant for the everyday control you need with your dog.

Your dog does not have to sit at each halt as is required in the AKC obedience ring. In competition the sits need to be near-perfect, quick, precise and straight. It is best that dogs learn precise heeling before sitting is added, if they are to compete. When I walk my dogs in public, I often prefer that they not automatically sit when we stop in the street. If the street is hot, icy cold or contaminated with fluid from cars, better that only the dog's feet be exposed. So, for either the someday obedience star or the recreational walker, not including an automatic sit on the heeling halts in the CGC Test is an advantage. It's okay if your dog does sit—and you can tell your dog "Sit" if you wish, since you are allowed to talk to your dog throughout the exercise.

10.5 WALK THROUGH A CROWD

In this portion of the test you use your loose-lead walking skills again, but this time you move with your dog around and close to at

On part four of the Canine Good Citizen Test, dog and handler walk through a "crowd" of at least three people, moving around and close to each of them.

Dash demonstrates part five of the test, which requires the dog to sit calmly at the handler's side and accept petting.

least three people. This demonstrates that your dog can maintain control around people and continue to work with you.

If you have trouble with this portion of the test, you and your dog need to practice! An obedience class would give you the needed opportunity to work your dog around others. Another approach is to *gradually* increase the degree of distraction as you practice with your dog on outings. In this exercise you would first master walking together in a quiet place, and then move on to slightly more distracting places to practice, with people at a distance. As the dog succeeds at that level, gradually move closer to the people for practice on subsequent days. It is particularly important to progress slowly if the dog is nervous about the other people. The dog deserves the opportunity to have enough life experience to learn that it can trust the situation before you take it to a test. Socialization is a long conditioning process that can be ruined by pushing the dog too rapidly.

10.6 SIT FOR EXAM

In this portion of the test the dog sits at the handler's left side while the Evaluator approaches the dog, pets it on the head and body, and circles dog and handler before moving away.

This quick, simple exercise checks that the dog will allow someone to approach it and pet it. In the initial examination of the dog by the Evaluator, the dog does not have to sit and could be taken up to the Evaluator rather than the Evaluator making the approach. Also, the handler could help hold the dog for the Evaluator to examine it. Now, however, the dog must hold steady on its own and tolerate being approached by a strange person and petted.

Some dogs feel threatened or nervous when someone approaches. It is more difficult for the dog than when it makes the approach to the person. If your dog has trouble with this, practice in low-pressure social settings, and help the dog learn to approach people for petting. As the dog gains confidence, it will feel less nervous about being approached by people. If the dog is small, early practice with the dog elevated on a table or other structure—or even in the handler's arms—can be a helpful step in overcoming the dog's fears.

For dogs that take the opposite view and want to jump up on the person and get petted sooner, practice sessions should include restraining the dog in the sitting position while it is being petted. After

190

Part six of the test requires the dog to "Sit" and "Down" on command. The handler may speak to the dog as much as desired but may not force the dog into position.

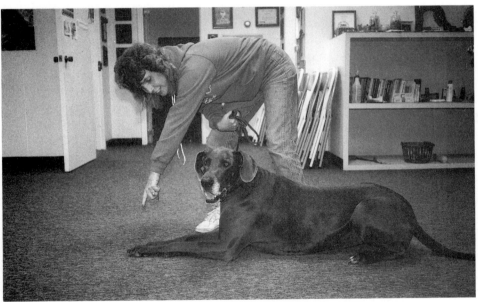

numerous repetitions over a period of perhaps weeks, the dog will learn that it must stay seated for petting. Don't be too rough with your handling of the dog to keep it sitting, as this may cause it to dislike people. Standing on the leash may be helpful. If the dog is too strong for you to restrain, get the help of a trainer. A very strong dog requires that the handler have some technical skill you really can't learn from a book. Anger and violence are not the answer—but that's what many dog owners resort to out of ignorance.

10.7 SIT AND DOWN ON COMMAND

For this portion of the test you will give your dog two commands, "Sit" and "Down." You do not have to get your dog to respond on the first command, and the Evaluator will give you some time. Some handlers who have not had ring experience will be flustered at having to get the dog to perform on command on the spot, but the Evaluator will probably reassure you that you don't have to rush. You simply have to demonstrate that your dog will Sit on command and Down on command, without you pushing or forcing the dog to take either position.

If you wish to work your dog in public, you need these two commands. The Sit and the Down help you "anchor" your dog to deal with various situations that arise when you are out together. One example of an appropriate time to have the dog sit is when waiting to cross a busy street. Your eyes are on the traffic and you need the dog steady at your side. A seated dog also indicates to drivers that your dog is under control.

The Down is necessary for situations when you need the dog even more securely anchored. One good example is when you are out for a walk and want to sit down, especially if you want to sit with other people and your dog is a large dog. Guide dogs for the blind are trained to lie down whenever the handler sits down, which is extremely practical. When I am seated and Saint is also seated, he is in a good position to poke his nose into my business, especially any food I'm trying to eat! Besides keeping the dog out of the food, having it lie down makes people around me feel more at ease. I use this command in public whenever people who seem uncomfortable have to pass near my dog and me. When Saint lies down they can see that he is under control and they feel less vulnerable.

Part seven gives the handler a choice of the "Sit" or "Down" position for the "Stay" command. The handler drops the leash and walks away. The dog must remain in place until the handler returns and releases it.

The Down position also requires your dog to submit to you. It is an excellent exercise to practice whenever you feel your dog is acting sassy. Instead of yelling or hitting, you just tell the dog to lie down and stay down until you say it may get up.

10.8 STAY IN POSITION (SIT OR DOWN)

For this exercise you are given the choice of commanding your dog to "Sit" or "Down" before you command it to "Stay" in that position. As in the previous section, you are allowed extra commands and a reasonable length of time to get your dog into the position, but you must not force the dog. On the Evaluator's instruction, you then command your dog to "Stay" and drop the leash and walk forward about twenty feet before you return to the dog at a natural pace. Your dog must stay until the Evaluator tells you to give it permission to move.

You might think that you would never, when out in public, tell your dog to "Stay" and drop the leash and walk away. However, if you spend much time with your dog in public, there are two circumstances you will eventually encounter that make this capability essential.

1. The leash will slip out of your hand. Suddenly your dog is not under your physical restraint. A good Stay command will save the day. This *will* happen to you sometime! I once witnessed a near-fatal incident when the lead attaching a little black dog to its owner slipped from the owner's hand and the dog continued to move at the same rate of speed toward a four-lane street, a couple of car lengths from a busy intersection. They weren't extremely close to the street when the lead slipped, but it seemed to take forever for him to catch up to the dog and he barely got there in time. When the same thing occasionally happens to me on a walk, I say "Wait" or "Stay," and my dog stops and waits while I pick up the leash. This control is essential. Everybody occasionally fumbles the leash, and they can break, too.
2. An emergency can arise. This can be any number of critical events when there is no time to tie your dog. Someone's life may be at risk, for instance, and you need the use of both

hands. If your dog knows a steady Stay command, there is a good chance you will not lose your dog in the process of dealing with a crisis. One common example of such a situation is when a small child starts to wander into traffic and no one but you is close enough to intervene.

Stay work demands that you provide your dog with adequate practice. Start by standing or sitting next to the dog as it stays for a few seconds before you release it. Work your way up over a period of weeks or months, until the dog will stay in a Sit position for perhaps two minutes or in a Down for about ten. Practice every day. When the dog breaks before you have released it, put it back into position with the gentlest handling that will work and restart the clock. Help the dog to succeed. Gradually, as the dog becomes more and more steady, move farther and farther away. At every practice, keep your eye on the time, so that the time you require your dog to Stay increases gradually and is consistent. Don't go from a one-minute Stay one day to a five-minute Stay the next. Add extra seconds every few days at first, and later you might be able to add an extra minute every week or so.

You can even train a mature dog to the point that you can go out of sight while it does a Stay. It is good training to do this. At first, when you go out of sight, peek at the dog, and let it see you. Later, you should always monitor the dog, either through some means where it cannot see you or through the use of an assistant. Otherwise there are dogs that will get up and wander around but be back in place before their handlers return, unaware that their dogs did not stay in place the entire time. Training is faster and better if you let the dog know just as soon as it makes a mistake that that is not the behavior you want. If you come back minutes later and the dog has left its Stay, there is no way to clearly explain to the dog that its mistake was at the moment it broke the Stay. The dog needs the correction, and on Stay work a verbal correction is often sufficient—at the right moment.

The Down is a more stable position than the Sit for times of real need. You may also wish to teach your dog to stay in a stand position for a minute so you can deal with situations such as stickers in its feet, and to reinforce your Stay when you drop the leash by accident as the dog is walking (in a standing position).

Stay practice need not be time-consuming, and it is extremely useful around the house as well as in public with your dog. "Stay" can stop your dog from jumping out of the car, from dashing through a gate or door when you or your guests exit, and from running through the house with dirty feet when it comes in from a trip outdoors. "Stay" can remind your dog not to misbehave at feeding time—the dog's feeding time *or* yours!

Every time you command your dog to "Stay," you accept the responsibility of remaining alert to release the dog at the proper time. Otherwise the dog will eventually figure out that you don't always remember, and it will begin releasing itself. Then you have lost your Stay command and have to build it back through practice. Return to your dog before releasing it and, for best results, teach it to hold steady for fifteen seconds after your return. One exception is when you say "Stay" to tell your dog not to exit a door with you. The dog will quickly learn that this is not a command to Stay after you've closed the door and gone!

You do not need a ten-minute Stay for this section of the CGC Test, but for some dogs you might, for the final section (the tie-out). If your dog displays the kind of agitation when left alone that the test is screening for, teach it a good out-of-sight Stay and you will solve the problem.

10.9   REACTION TO ANOTHER DOG

For many dogs this will be the most difficult portion of the test, and for their owners it may be the most educational. It is a common misconception that aggressiveness toward other dogs is not a real problem because people think it poses no danger to humans. In fact many people are injured when dogs fight with one another, and a few little children have even been killed. If you intend to take your dog out in public, you must be able to pass this portion of the test.

What you are required to do is approach and shake hands with another handler while both of you have dogs at your sides. Your dog is required to accept this situation with the same attitude as when the Evaluator approached earlier in the CGC Test and shook your hand. After the two handlers shake hands, they each continue on for a short distance. This tests your dog face to face with another dog, as well as its reaction to a dog moving toward it and then away from it.

When you take this test, the other dog will be under control and your own dog will have come through the previous seven sections of

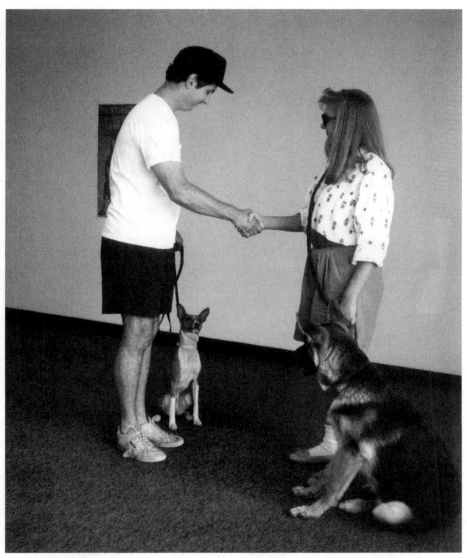

Part eight of the Canine Good Citizen Test demonstrates your dog's reaction to another dog as you and the other handler shake hands.

the test. Thus, the Evaluator will know that your dog is under reasonable control before allowing you to try this. In daily life out in public with your dog, however, the other dog may be off-leash (much as we wish that would never happen), and it may be a dog that wishes to fight with your dog. Considering what you may face in controlling your dog around other dogs in the real world, this test is tame!

If your dog tends to misbehave around other dogs, attend an obedience class where the dog will be exposed to other dogs repeatedly—with the other dogs on-leash—and will learn to tolerate it. If the misbehavior is aggressiveness, discuss it with the instructor before enrolling. If the instructor requires you to take private lessons before enrolling the dog in a class, it will be time well spent. Be honest with the instructor and get the help you need. Otherwise, it is not safe to take the dog-aggressive dog out in public.

10.10   REACTIONS TO DISTRACTIONS

On this portion of the test your dog will experience two distractions chosen at the Evaluator's discretion from a list of distractions acceptable to the AKC. These include someone dropping a large book no closer than ten feet behind your dog; the sudden closing or opening of a door; a jogger running in front of your dog; people good-naturedly pushing and shoving each other and slapping each other's backs within ten feet of where you and your dog pass; someone approaching your dog and passing about six feet to the side with a shopping cart; a person riding by on a bicycle; and a person using a wheelchair, crutches or a walker. I have experienced every one of these things when out on walks with my dogs, and you will experience at least some of them if you frequently walk with your dog. If the dog cannot remain under your control when such things happen, disaster could result when you are out in public with it.

The dog does not have to remain stock-still or show no reaction at all. It may startle, show curiosity, or otherwise be affected by the distractions as long as it does not panic, behave aggressively, or go out of control.

If your dog has trouble with distractions such as these, the solution is to first practice your control work, such as heeling, staying and other commands, at a distance from such activities. Then, over many sessions, gradually move your practice closer and closer to the distrac-

Dropping a heavy book is one of the possible distractions used on part nine of the test.

Lady is unconcerned about these romping children—a good-natured, slightly rowdy group of people is another possible distraction for the test.

tions. If at any time the dog behaves aggressively, seek the help of an instructor. Most dogs simply need to find out in a nonthreatening way and over a long, nonstressful period of time that these things will not hurt them. They need to learn through experience that they will be safe as long as they obey their handlers' commands, and that they can trust their handlers never to give commands that will put them in danger.

10.11 DOG LEFT ALONE

In the final exercise, you fasten your dog to a fifteen-foot line and go out of sight for five minutes while the Evaluator watches over your dog. The dog should remain calm and quiet, but will still pass the test if it moves slightly—it is not required to do a Stay.

You may not appreciate the usefulness of this exercise until you come across a dog that can't do it! Some dogs promptly launch themselves into conniption fits when their owners walk out of sight. In such a state they may try to burrow through doors, break or chew through their tethers if they are tied, upset the neighborhood with their noise, and cause other destruction. But perhaps even more important is that they are not happy and they do not feel secure.

If you are out in public and for some reason need to tie your dog and step away from it—whether out of sight or not—it is imperative that your dog remain calm and quiet. Otherwise it disturbs others, endangers itself, and may even agitate other dogs nearby who are not tied. This could lead to a dogfight that otherwise would not have occurred. You surely do not want your dog to suffer in this manner.

Some dogs will learn the tie-out easily: temperament factors as well as experiences the dogs have had will determine the difficulty. You can make this into an out-of-sight Down-Stay with the added security of the tie-out as an anchor. If your dog is either an insecure type or a bossy type, giving it the specific assignment of remaining in the Down-Stay may be necessary for it to pass the test. It is difficult for a dog to make noise and behave in an agitated manner while maintaining a Down-Stay. The command also gives the dog a focus, rather than worrying about where you have gone and when you are coming back.

Whether or not you choose to teach the exercise as a Stay, practice by building your time gradually. First get the dog accustomed to being tied with you there. You might lead the dog to the limits of the tether

In the final exercise, "Dog Left Alone," your dog must remain calm on a fifteen-foot line while you go out of sight for five minutes.

The Canine Good Citizen team has the skills for pleasant daily walks, as well as many other activities that untrained dogs and their owners cannot safely enjoy.

and let it experience them under control, so the restraint won't frighten it later if it moves on its own.

After the dog is comfortable on the tether with you in sight, begin going out of sight for gradually increasing lengths of time. Work until you almost always stay away for at least six minutes (but not more than ten) before you take the test. Then on the test when you return in five minutes, it will seem shorter than normal for the dog and will reduce stress. If you were to practice for more than ten minutes, you might lead your dog to think the test was going to be really tough, and some dogs might give up and break control, especially if something causes the dog to become stressed while you are away. So make sure your practice does not make the dog worry that you will be gone much longer than you actually will.

On this portion of the test, as well as the exercise that tests your dog's reaction to another dog, you are placing a great deal of faith in the Evaluator not to endanger your dog. Satisfy yourself before the test begins that the Evaluator is worthy of being entrusted with your dog's safety. In real life you would not leave your dog tied and unattended in a public place. The dog would be with someone you trust—in this case, the Evaluator—or in your sight.

When you practice the tie-out or the formal Stay command, you are making a promise to your dog that you will come back. If you always keep that promise in practice, the dog will have confidence in you on the test—as well as in real life—and your chances of success will be greatly increased.

10.12 FOR *ALL* DOGS AND OWNERS: A TOOL FOR RESPONSIBLE DOG OWNERSHIP

The Canine Good Citizen Test is open to mixed-breed dogs as well as registered and unregistered purebreds. That makes it a truly American test, democratic with the same opportunity for all! It takes only a few minutes to administer to each dog, and does not require a specific type of location or expensive equipment. Some obedience classes use it as a graduation test. Other groups offer it as part of other events. Recently the AKC authorized modifications to use the test as a screening device for therapy dogs. When the event is one that is open to all dogs, the test is also open to all dogs. But it can also be given at events where participation is limited to dogs of a particular breed or other special group, or where pre-entry is required. There does not even have to be an event—one dog can be tested at a time, as long as the necessary people and another dog are available for the test.

The flexibility of the Canine Good Citizen Test creates many possibilities for using it to educate and inspire people about responsible dog ownership, as well as what training can accomplish. At this writing it appears likely that there will, in future, be a more advanced test offered, one designed to give dog owners a goal to work toward after the Canine Good Citizen Test.

One thing I enjoy about the test and about watching others take it is that much of the individuality of the dog and of the handler show in the way they work. Obedience competitors have to behave in a standardized manner, since any deviation from precise perfection is points off. On the Canine Good Citizen Test you see handlers encourage their dogs, praise them while they work rather than just between exercises, and show their own personalities. The Evaluator, too, gets more personally involved than does the judge at an obedience trial (who is under strict time constraints) and has more opportunity to educate the dog owner during the test. The same rule about not mistreating the dog exists for both activities, which makes observing pleasant and unmarred by watching people abuse their dogs. Several parts of the Canine Good Citizen Test offer a second chance, which the competition obedience ring does not. Second chances are inspiring.

If you have in the past been less than responsible as a dog owner, take this second chance. Use what you have learned in this book to make life better for your dog, your neighbors and yourself. Dogs have an incredible capacity to forgive, adapt and learn new ways of life. It's not too late to make things right. In dealing with dogs we relate to living creatures, and where there is life, there is hope.